Service Oriented Architecture Field Guide for Executives

Service Oriented Architecture Field Guide for Executives

Kyle Gabhart

Bibhas Bhattacharya

WILEY

John Wiley & Sons, Inc.

Library of Congress Cataloging-in-Publication Data:

Gabhart, Kyle, 1979-
   Service oriented architecture field guide for executives/
Kyle Gabhart, Bibhas Bhattacharya.
        p. cm.
   Includes index.
   ISBN 978-0-470-26091-3 (cloth)
   1. Information technology–Management. 2. Computer architecture. I. Bhattacharya, Bibhas, 1967- II. Title.
   HD30.2.G33 2008
   004.068–dc22
2008009614

Printed in the United States of America

10 9 8 7 6 5 4 3 2 1

To my son, Gabriel, my parents, and the entire Wheeler family—Bibhas
To my best friend Elizabeth, daughter Kati, and two troublemakers,
Alex and Drew—Kyle

CONTENTS

Preface   *ix*

Acknowledgments   *xi*

SECTION ONE: WHAT IS SOA AND WHY
SHOULD I CARE?   1

CHAPTER 1
SOA Primer   3

CHAPTER 2
Business Process Management and SOA   29

CHAPTER 3
SOA Value Proposition   59

CHAPTER 4
Risks in SOA Adoption   73

SECTION TWO: IS SOA RIGHT FOR MY BUSINESS?   95

CHAPTER 5
Is SOA Right for You?   97

CHAPTER 6
Applying SOA to Various Industries   107

CHAPTER 7
Calculating SOA ROI   125

SECTION THREE: HOW SHOULD I GO ABOUT
ADOPTING SOA?   141

CHAPTER 8
Selecting an SOA Maturity Model   143

CHAPTER 9
How Much SOA Do I Need?   161

CHAPTER 10
Acquiring the Skills for SOA   175

CHAPTER 11
Risk Mitigation through Proper Governance   187

CHAPTER 12
Creating Your SOA Adoption Plan   199

Appendix   Standards in SOA   *211*

Index   *223*

PREFACE

This book began its journey in June 2005 when Web Age Solutions delivered its first customized *service oriented architecture (SOA)* education program. As the standard and custom curriculum developed and mentoring engagements ensued, best practices and enterprise-level implications for service orientation began to emerge. Executive-level overviews of SOA were offered in 2006, as well as architect and developer bootcamps. In 2007, Web Age produced several whitepapers around SOA and expanded its curriculum to include a broader set of roles, increased focus on enterprise strategy and executive decision making, and industry-centric solution offerings. This book builds on this body of work and incorporates frameworks, methodologies, best practices, and guidance that have been honed based on real-life experiences with clients of all shapes and sizes from a wide range of industries and market segments.

Throughout our client engagements and participation at various conferences, a very real gap between the business and technology communities made itself apparent. Massive resources are available to technologists who wish to pursue SOA. A smaller set of resources are available to senior analysts and managers who wish to pursue SOA. Virtually no resources exist to provide business leaders, technology executives, or other key innovators with guidance regarding what SOA is really about, when it makes sense, when it does not, and how to pragmatically go about evaluating and ultimately adopting it. We wrote this book to fill that void.

ACKNOWLEDGMENTS

Writing this book has been a journey and a labor of love for both of us. This text is the result of years of developing and supporting service oriented solutions, working with our clients on their service oriented strategies, and countless hours of research. The strategies, frameworks, models, and guidelines outlined in this book are not theoretical. They are applied daily by us and the entire Web Age team in classrooms, server rooms, and boardrooms throughout North America and around the world.

Of course, this book could not have been written without the support of an incredible team behind us. Thanks are due to several people who supported the book as advisors and reviewers: Jason Bloomberg, Lisa Bromwell, Paul Curtis, Ron Schmeltzer, and Chris White. We would like to thank the entire Web Age team for helping us by reviewing early drafts and providing us with valuable insight and critical feedback as this book came together. Special thanks to Tapas Banerjee, Greg Wagner, and Gary Bilodeau at Web Age for being flexible and supportive of our limited availability during the months that we spent writing this book.

Bibhas would like to extend special thanks to Tapas Banerjee and Stephen Wheeler. Both are thinkers in the areas of large-scale software development and IT management. Their feedback during lengthy and rather one-sided conversations with Bibhas provided valuable input for the book.

Kyle would like to thank Jason Gordon for introducing him to Java and XML, Chris White for helping him realize that there is more to life than Java (and for countless technical support calls at all hours of the night), and Kelly Johnson for taking a chance on a budding technologist so many years ago. Special thanks go out to Kyle's supportive parents, beautiful children Kati, Alex, and Drew, faithful dog Ginger, and partner and soul mate, Elizabeth. This book couldn't have happened without your love, support, and patience.

WHAT IS SOA AND WHY SHOULD I CARE?

If you haven't heard about *service oriented architecture (SOA),* then you have likely been living under a rock for the past several years (it is also very unlikely that you would purchase a book on the topic). There is a tremendous degree of hype, FUD (fear, uncertainty, and doubt), and misinformation floating around regarding SOA, service orientation in general, and what it really means for modern enterprises. This first part of the book is aimed at cutting through all of this and providing a solid foundation in SOA, its huge potential, and its inherent risks.

Chapter 1, "SOA Primer," introduces and defines SOA, explains what it means to be service oriented, and describes how we evolved to this point. The chapter introduces the typical architectural layers that comprise an SOA enterprise solution and the key SOA infrastructure elements that are commonly found.

Chapter 2, "Business Process Management and SOA," introduces and defines business process management (BPM), explains what it means to be process-centric, and describes how all of this relates to SOA. Alignment between IT and business through BPM is examined, along with the relationship between objects, services, and processes. Finally, process modeling is explored in great detail.

Chapter 3, "SOA Value Proposition," identifies the four core SOA value propositions (reduced integration expense, increased asset reuse, business agility, reduced risk) as well as several emerging values (alignment, time to market, visibility, and modernization). These value propositions are then explored by looking at the two fictitious case studies used throughout this book.

Chapter 4, "Risks in SOA Adoption," takes a raw and honest look at IT challenges and barriers to SOA success. Common SOA promises are examined, including business and IT alignment, process automation through SOA, service reuse, service composition like LEGO® blocks, smoother integration through open standards, and improved business responsiveness. SOA has potential, but this chapter provides a very real look at the risks inherent within SOA.

CHAPTER I

SOA PRIMER

You awake to the familiar buzz of your alarm clock and stumble out of bed and into the bathroom. With a flick of a light switch you are blinded by the bathroom light (unless you have one of those fancy bathroom lights that gradually brightens to allow your eyes to adjust). Later you plug in your coffee grinder, grind some fresh beans, and then brew a steaming pot of coffee. Throughout your morning routine, you use electricity. You use as much or as little of it as you need and you do so with little regard for how much electricity you have consumed that day, week, or month. Some weeks or months, travel and work schedule may dictate less time at home (and less electricity consumption); other days or weeks, you may consume much more. Electricity is a service. It is available on-demand based on a predetermined fee structure and is delivered consistently based on industry standards and regulated infrastructure. Electricity, like other utilities, is service oriented.

FROM AD-HOC SOLUTIONS TO SERVICE ORIENTED CAPABILITIES

At first glance, *service oriented architecture (SOA)* sounds like a techie thing with little relevance to business and delivering customer value. But service orientation is more than just a technical architecture; it is a movement within government organizations and private industry that is transforming business value chains, organizational alignment, and technical delivery capabilities.

To better understand this transition, we will first examine the evolution within the electric utility industry from ad-hoc creation of electricity toward a true service oriented model. Then we will explore the parallels currently occurring within the realms of business and technology with respect to SOA.

Edison Had a Neat Idea

Generating electricity to illuminate a bulb is a pretty cool concept. The means of getting the electricity to the bulb has evolved over time. Creating that electricity via generators was a fine initial implementation, but that method was not as economical or reliable as desired. Generators required individuals and businesses to stockpile fuel in order to produce electricity. They also had limited ability to regulate the electricity flow, resulting in reliability problems as well as safety concerns. Later, the electricity needs of towns and cities were supported by power plants. Generation of power within homes and businesses gave way to transmission of power from centralized plants via electrical lines. Eventually, these plants connected with one another via a standardized power grid, enabling the exchange of power supply across great distances. Power demand could now be supplied by plants in other regions via the power grid. As demand changes, individual plants can throttle the supply of power, enabling the entire grid to respond to market needs.

There is another interesting aspect to the electric power industry, and that is the *economics of deregulation*. Although in some parts of the world electric service is owned or at least heavily regulated by the government, others have deregulated and embraced a free-market model. In these deregulated markets, private industry can build a plant, generate electricity, connect to the grid, and negotiate service levels and a price to sell this electricity to brokers. Industry standards, transmission protocols, and robust infrastructure enable a truly service oriented industry in which demand can wax and wane, supply can be delivered from anywhere on the grid, and new providers can enter the market and negotiate price and service level agreements (SLAs) as needed.

Service Orienting Modern Enterprises Is a Good Idea, Too

From localized generation of electricity to transmission of electricity from centralized power plants to distribution of electricity via a power grid, the electric utility industry has evolved into a service oriented model. As illustrated in Exhibit 1.1, this same evolution is taking place in modern enterprises today. Originally, businesses deployed local software (applications and databases) and hardware (personal computers and servers) to support business operations. Large, distributed businesses would require multiple instances of such software. Later, network infrastructure and distributed computing technologies allowed businesses to deploy centralized solutions (software and hardware) with distributed client-side access in lieu of multiple copies of the full software/hardware stack. These centralized solutions are much more economical and more powerful than having a bunch of solutions deployed in every location. The drawback, however, is that these solutions are not flexible. They offer a monolithic, one-size-fits-all solution. If you need to tweak one aspect of business operations (e.g., modify your

EXHIBIT **1.1** *As with the electric industry, the computing industry has evolved into a service oriented model*

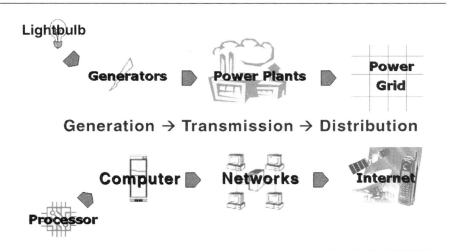

supply chain process, change the data processing logic for one product type, outsource one component of the application, etc.), you generally have to go through a long design–development–testing–deployment life cycle. Service orientation is about taking those monolithic solutions and breaking them up into flexible, reusable, and configurable components. These components, or services, are available to service requests from anywhere in the network without the traditional barriers of operating system, programming language, or platform technology. Additionally, these can be reconfigured and a chain of services rearranged in a fraction of the time that traditional solutions can be changed in order to respond to changing business needs. To return to our electric utility industry analogy, service orientation allows enterprises to respond more readily to electricity demand (service requests) and to adjust power supplied by power plants (reconfigure service providers) to adjust to the demands of the grid (network).

Finally, there is the issue of economics and deregulation. Just as a deregulated power industry permits new providers to join the grid and sell power to customers, so, too, does a service oriented enterprise model. The key in both cases is industry standards, transmission protocols, and robust infrastructure. By service orienting the enterprise, businesses introduce the potential to connect systems and databases within their internal enterprise and even connect to trusted partners and third-party service providers. Why maintain an address cleanup capability when you can simply invoke address services maintained by the U.S. Postal Service (or similar national postal service)? Why maintain your own geographical tracking and management capabilities when you can simply call services made available by Google Maps? Service orientation allows business needs to be fulfilled by any provider within the local or extended network, provided that they support the appropriate technology standards, message transmission protocols, and required SLAs. On-demand, service oriented capabilities, backed by service contracts and enforceable SLAs—imagine scaling your business, meeting increasing customer demands, and doing so as effortlessly as you turn on a light bulb.

WHAT EXACTLY IS SOA?

In exploring SOA, we will start by defining the concept and then look at some of the most common components that comprise SOA solutions.

Defining SOA

SOA can be expressed very simply:

> SOA is about connecting customer requirements with enterprise capabilities, regardless of technology landscape or arbitrary organizational boundaries.

Digging in further, we learn that SOA means different things to different people. At a very low level, it is a technical architecture supported by standard formats and protocols. At a more general level, it represents a shift within the enterprise toward breaking up organizational silos and monolithic information systems to enable flexibility in how customer solutions are assembled. Chiefly, SOA aims to align technology investments and initiatives with business goals through an enterprise governance plan.

In some respects, the *A* in *SOA* is a bit unfortunate. While architecture is certainly a key aspect of any successful SOA initiative, it tends to give the erroneous impression that SOA is an "IT thing" that the business community need not worry about. The reality is that service orientation is an enterprise strategy with far-reaching implications into business capabilities, organization structure, technical infrastructure, and the overall agility and efficiency of enterprise operations. Consequently, a distinction will be made in this text between SOA (a style of enterprise architecture) and service orientation (an enterprise strategy that focuses on business processes, serving customers, and alignment of enterprise resources with business objectives).

DECONSTRUCTING SOA

No two service oriented enterprise architectures look the same. SOA is an architectural style with a handful of common elements and themes and myriad implementation strategies. A nominal, representative

architecture can be identified in order to better understand SOA and
"what it looks like." A reference diagram depicting the SOA layers is
illustrated in Exhibit 1.2. This diagram will serve as a useful reference
in this section and throughout the rest of the book. While any given
implementation of SOA may be more or less complex than this model,
this diagram provides a good starting place.

The layers illustrated in Exhibit 1.2 are as follows:[1]

- **Operational resources.** Comprised of existing systems, applications, and databases, the operational resources layer represents
  the legacy enterprise. Your customer relationship management
  (CRM), enterprise resource planning (ERP), and product life-cycle
  management (PLM) systems are good examples of operational resources. Some of these systems are commercial off-the-shelf

EXHIBIT **1.2** *SOA architectural layers*

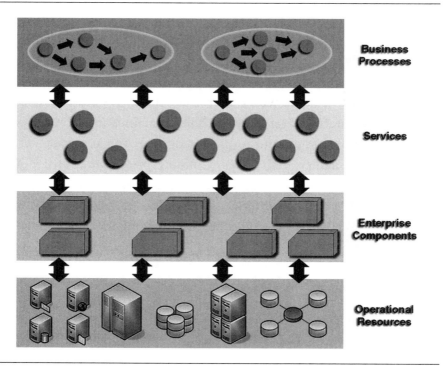

(COTS), while others are homegrown, but all of them house valuable enterprise data and business logic. The services that are made available through an SOA leverage these existing investments and uncover new opportunities for utilizing these assets within a larger enterprise context.

- **Enterprise components.** Sitting atop the operational resources is a layer of enterprise components. Enterprise components typically employ container-based technologies such as CORBA, EJB, COM, DCOM, .NET, and the like. These assets are responsible for managing custom business logic and interfacing with the operational resource layer to carry out this logic. Additionally, they support the scalability and quality-of-service requirements of the services exposed in the layer above. A service's ability to support contracted SLAs is based on how well designed the enterprise component layer is that supports the service.

- **Services.** Capabilities from the enterprise component layer are selectively identified as services. The analysis, design, and development of these services is then funded and the services are deployed in order to expose these capabilities through well-defined interfaces. Service descriptions, quality-of-service (QoS) SLAs, and other key service metadata are also defined to accompany these important SOA assets.

- **Business processes.** Individual services provide incremental value for an organization but will likely never transform the way business gets done. Business processes, however, represent powerful orchestrations of one or more services that solve a business problem. Services are bundled together into a logical flow (described as *orchestration* or *choreography*) to solve some sort of end-to-end business problem. For example, one service might provide access into the purchase order mechanism for an ERP system and another provide access into customer account capabilities within the CRM system, but a business process could lump these services and perhaps others together in order to complete an order fulfillment request.

Key Infrastructure Elements

Just as every SOA is likely to be different, the infrastructure that enables that architecture will also vary. There are, however, some common components and SOA infrastructure pieces that you are likely to encounter when exploring SOA enterprise solutions. These include:

- **Business rules engine.** This allows business logic to be defined in such a way as to enable business owners (especially the line of business managers) to tweak and throttle key variables that drive certain business processes. Examples include tweaking insurability thresholds in the insurance industry and throttling service performance to respond to increasing seasonal demand in the retail industry.

- **Enterprise Service Bus (ESB).** Considered by some to be the quintessential SOA infrastructure element, an ESB can be used to broker service transactions, map interfaces and data sets (enabling clients and services with differing expectations to communicate seamlessly), route traffic to appropriate services based on internal logic, and perform other value-added service-brokering solutions.

- **Policy server.** Governing SOA to ensure that business objectives are met and that the enterprise is not exposed to undue risk is crucial. One mechanism for governing SOA is through the definition and implementation of policies, which are then applied to business processes as well as individual services. Policies will be discussed at length in Chapter 11, but essentially represent declarations regarding the use of service data and metadata or other nonfunctional qualities such as performance, security, or service reliability.

- **Service container.** This is where the services actually live. Resource pooling and intelligent caching may be implanted here to improve performance. This is typically some sort of application server and may, in fact, be bundled into an ESB platform.

- **Process engine.** This supports the definition, configuration, and execution of business processes (service orchestrations), and manages these processes and invokes service operations to fulfill process activities in a well-defined sequence. It may exist as a standalone installation or be bundled within an ESB platform.

- **Service manager.** The service manager is responsible for service life-cycle management, monitoring service health and performance, client access tracking, and in some cases even enforcing policies and SLAs. The service manager may also manage service versioning. Finally, it might exist as a standalone installation or be bundled with a service container, a policy server, an ESB platform, or any combination thereof.

- **Service registry/repository.** With few exceptions, this infrastructure element will exist for every SOA enterprise. Depending on the size and requirements of the enterprise, any of the previously identified infrastructure elements may or may not exist. The registry/repository is crucial, because it serves as the directory for service descriptions, interfaces, and other key metadata. Services also can be organized within the registry/repository according to a predefined or organization-specific taxonomy or categorization schemes to support service discovery. Some registries/repositories are deployed independently, while others are bundled with a service manager, policy manager, ESB, or some combination thereof.

IS SOA THE LATEST INDUSTRY FAD?

The pace of change within the business community, and information technology in particular, rightly leads the savvy professional to question whether SOA is merely a fad. Technologies and trends come and go, so what makes SOA any different? Several factors point to SOA's longevity.

SOA Is a Natural Evolution

To start with, service orientation evolved out of mature application and integration efforts in the late 1990s, and came on the scene around 2000–2001. Since that time, the adoption of Web Services and service orientation among vendors and private industry has been tremendous (some research pegs the number as high as 90% among Fortune 500s). Federal and state governments are even engaging in early service oriented initiatives. Virtually every vendor of enterprise systems now has an SOA initiative to one degree or another. Some enterprises are able to jumpstart their SOA efforts merely by upgrading to the latest releases for their major COTS systems. Even CICS mainframes have gotten on the bandwagon. The latest version of CICS includes native support for Web Services. This is, in fact, the trend throughout the industry.

SOA Has Staying Power

All indicators point to SOA remaining a viable and lasting part of the enterprise. Consider the following quote from Gartner in a November 2006 research note:[2]

> SOA will be a *durable change* in application architecture, more like the relational data model than shorter-lived concepts, such as distributed object computing using object request brokers.

By placing service orientation alongside the other major shifts in information technology (IT) (see Exhibit 1.3[3]), the significance of its impact is made even clearer.

EXHIBIT **1.3** *Service orientation represents a major shift in enterprise computing*

Approach	Time Frame	Programming Model	Business Motivations
Mainframe timesharing	1960s–1980s	Procedural (COBOL)	Automated business
Client/server	1980s–1990s	Database (SQL) and fat client (VB, Powerbuilder, etc.)	Computing power on the desktop
N-Tier/Web	1990s–2000s	Object-oriented (Java, PHP, COM, etc.)	Internet/eBusiness
Service orientation	2000s	Message-oriented (XML)	Business Agility

SUMMARY

Service orientation is a powerful concept and represents a business model that has been successful in a variety of industries (most notably the electric utility industry). Enterprises are in the process of evaluating service orientation and considering the potential that it holds for transforming the way business gets done and enabling an alignment between IT goals and business goals. Although the hype cycle is in full swing, there exist some tangible motivations and real-world value behind SOA. Throughout the remainder of this book, the subjects of service orientation and business alignment will be examined with a careful eye to identifying how a savvy business leader can determine when SOA makes sense and when it does not.

SOA CASE STUDIES

A few examples will help you look at service oriented architecture (SOA) in proper context. Here, we will present two case studies. They will give you an idea of the type of business problems SOA is good at solving. We will also discuss the general solution approach.

Right off the bat, you will notice that these problems cannot be solved by software alone. You will need people, machines, and software all playing roles in a well-defined business process.

Case Study A: Return Handling

Retail companies have been accepting sold goods back from their clients for a long time. This operation is generally called *return handling, goods inflow*, or *reverse inventory*. The case study presented here is based on the work done by de Koster et al.[4]

General Background Information

MO1 is a mail-order retail company. It sells electronic goods, such as television sets, home theater systems, CDs, DVDs and cables. MO1 runs an e-commerce web site where customers can place orders. MO1 also releases printed catalogues and accepts orders over the phone.

Mail-order companies experience a high rate of return. This is true for MO1. Customers return about 15% of the goods sold. About 20% of the warehouse space is dedicated toward returns handling.

Current Business Operation

Products can be returned within 30 days of delivery. MO1 offers full satisfaction guarantee. If, for any reason, a customer is not happy with a product, all she has to do is call the customer support line. If the dissatisfaction is due to a perceived technical problem, customer support does its best to resolve them. If the customer confirms her decision to return, the customer service representative logs the reason for return and provides the customer with a return address.

All returns are sent to a warehouse. When a package arrives, a staff member locates the call center log for the order to find out why the product is being returned. What MO1 does with the returned products depends on the reason for return. Exhibit 1.4 summarizes the actions.

Exhibit 1.5 shows the current business process in a graphical form. A business process manager or analyst will typically model the business process this way using graphical notations.

The Problems

Overall, MO1 needs to lower the cost of return handling and minimize errors. Specifically, the following problems exist in the current operation:

- When a returned package is received, it takes a staff member several minutes to locate the order details and the call center log. The staff attempts to locate the information by searching for the customer's name and address.
- Staff member has to manually enter the same data in several systems. These systems include call center, warehouse management

EXHIBIT **1.4** *List of reasons customers return items and the actions taken by the MO1 staff based on the reason for return*

Reason for Return	Action
Product does not meet customer's need or expectation of quality. Product itself is not defective.	Product is touched up, repackaged, and returned back to shelf. The inventory on hand is incremented in the warehouse system.
Product is defective.	Return product to the manufacturer if the manufacturer accepts defective goods. Otherwise, discard product and book it in the accounting system as loss.
Product was damaged during shipping and handling.	File a claim with the shipping provider if the shipment was insured. Otherwise, discard product and book it in the accounting system as loss.

system, manufacturer's web site, shipping carrier's web site, and the accounting system. This slows down the operation and introduces errors.

- Some of the defective items are sent back to the manufacturer. Staff member had made mistakes when preparing the package for shipment to the manufacturer. Shipping label has been printed with the address of the wrong manufacturer.
- Currently, staff members log into the accounting system and initiate refund to the customer. This has led to errors and in some cases malpractice.

Improvement Opportunities

MO1 has identified several areas of improvement:

- It is generally believed that certain products have a higher rate of return. This may have to do with the way the product is represented in the web site or the printed catalogue. MO1 would like to know which products have a high return rate so that appropriate

Exhibit **1.5** *The as-is business process*

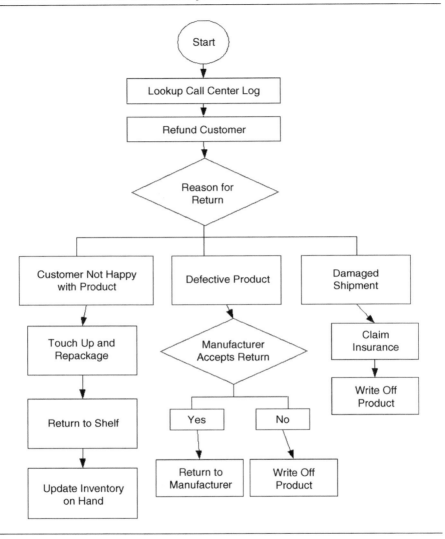

changes can be made to the description and photograph of the product.

- For some of the cheaper items, processing the return costs more than the item itself. In these cases, items could be simply scrapped.
- Return processing can be considerably sped up with a better-designed warehouse workflow and more efficient sorting process

for returned packages. The main focus area here will be integration between different systems, which will eliminate the need for duplicate data entry.

How Can SOA Help?

Can SOA really help MO1 devise a solution?

SOA takes a much more complete view of the business problem than traditional approaches like object-oriented analysis and design (OOAD). SOA attempts to solve a problem by using a combination of employees, resources such as software applications, machines, factories, and business partners.

In a sense, SOA cannot be presented as merely a software development methodology. It is an overall problem-solving approach. It involves the entire business in building a solution.

Now, let us have a look at how one follows the SOA approach to solve these problems.

First, SOA requires that you take a close look at the business process. In case of MO1, the current return handling process is highly inefficient and prone to many errors. By performing *business process management* (BPM), we will be able to improve the process quite a bit. (BPM is discussed in more detail in Chapter 2, Business Process Management and SOA).

After MO1 redesigned the business process, the following improvements were made:

- In the packages shipped to the customers, include a label that should be used as the return address. This makes customers' lives easier. More important, the label contains a bar code identifying the order. When the returned package is received at the warehouse, the staff simply scans the bar code. There is no longer any need to search for the order using the customer's name and address.
- Once the bar code is scanned, the system should automatically pull up the call center log for the order. Staff member does not have to log into the call center application and search for the order.

- Staff member enters the reason for return in a database. This is later analyzed to fix problems such as errors in the web site.
- The workflow should automatically contact the accounting software and initiate refund.
- If the product is defective and the manufacturer accepts returns, the system should automatically send an invoice to the manufacturer and print the correct shipping label. All the staff members have to do is slap that label on the package and move it to the shipping section of the warehouse.
- If the package was damaged during shipping, the system should automatically file a claim with the shipping carrier.

In SOA, the business process itself executes as a software. It can automate many tasks, for example, pulling up the call center log and initiating a refund with the accounting system. The employees do not have to log into all kinds of different software applications and manually enter data.

Next, SOA requires that you formally identify the players in the process. They are called *service providers* or simply *services*. In the return handling process, the employees, the web site, the call center application, the accounting system, the manufacturer, and the shipping carrier are the services.

Each service performs a set of tasks. For example, the accounting system can be asked to refund the credit card used for an order. The shipping carrier can be asked to accept an insurance claim for damaged goods. The staff members accept returned packages, do touchups, and repackage. They also place items in good condition back on the shelf.

Exhibit 1.6 shows a list of services in the return handling process and the tasks they perform.

Once services are identified, their roles and responsibilities become very clear. SOA now requires you to look for ways to automate tasks. Task automation can significantly reduce error and cost.

If a service provider is a software, such as the accounting system, it is relatively easy to automate the tasks. Essentially a task is automated by developing the software for the service that performs that task.

EXHIBIT **1.6** *Example services identified from the return handling process. Each service shows a set of operations that it is capable of performing*

Call Center • Locate call log for order	**Accounting System** • Refund customer • Write off product
Warehouse System • Increase inventory • Get product shelf location	**Manufacturer** • Do you accept return? • Return product
Staff • Determine return reason • Touch up and repackage	

If the service provider is a human being, we need to look for ways to use software to automate the task. For example, we could have the system automatically launch the call center application and pull up the call log and order history before an employee begins processing a return. Not all human tasks can be automated. SOA and BPM recognize this reality and support human-based services as well.

The shipping carrier and manufacturers are external organizations. They may or may not offer software services to automate the tasks. If they do, you need to consider using them instead of using their web sites, phone, or fax to ask them to do these tasks. For example, if the shipping carrier offers a Web Service to file an insurance claim, we should consider using that.

Once all the services are implemented (either by using software or by assigning staff members the relevant tasks), we can develop orchestration. *Orchestration* is a software program that controls the sequence of tasks in a process. Each task is performed by a service. With orchestration, human beings no longer manage the flow of activities in a business. For example, if a product has been returned because it was damaged during shipping, the orchestration will automatically ask the shipping carrier service to file a claim. The orchestration knows the context, which is the original order placed by the customer. As a result, it can automatically fetch all the information required by the shipping carrier, such as the waybill number and the account number.

Exhibit 1.7 shows what an orchestration looks like. Usually, software developers take the business process model created by the process

EXHIBIT **1.7** *A snippet of the return handling orchestration*

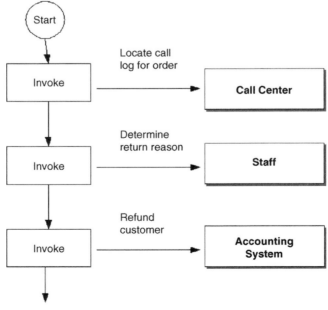

managers or analysts and convert that into orchestration. Orchestration uses the Invoke activity to ask a service to perform a specific task.

MO1 wishes to get a better understanding about the return handling process. To aid that, we can define *key performance indicators* (KPIs) for the orchestration. For MO1 the relevant KPIs are:

- Percentage distribution of reason for return.
- The top products getting returned because they do not meet customers' expectations of quality or do not meet their needs.
- How long it takes end-to-end from the time a returned package is received to the time it is fully processed. This will give some idea about how well the process is working.

Solution Summary

This completes our fictitious project where we follow the SOA approach to solve the problems of MO1. As you can see, SOA is not a technology, but a mindset for designing a solution. What follows is a summary of what we did:

- We used BPM to scrutinize the current business process. We found several ways to make it more error-proof and faster.
- We identified the roles and responsibilities of each service provider. Then we looked for ways to automate the tasks. We did that by developing services. Task automation can further speed up the operation and reduce error.
- We developed an orchestration. This will oversee the sequence of tasks. Orchestration has a twofold advantage. It helps with automation. It can also capture key statistical data known as KPIs, which help us get a better understanding about the business and improve its operations.

Case Study B: Expense Approval

This case study shows how SOA can play a role in a small company or for a small project. HighTree is a fictitious company that provides information technology (IT) training to Fortune 1000 companies. It employs several full-time and contracted teachers who travel to the training locations. These resources claim expenses incurred while they are on the road. HighTree has not been doing a very good job paying these claims on time or accurately. We will see how SOA can be used to improve the company's performance.

Current Business Operation

Currently, a teacher files an expense by sending an e-mail to the salesperson. The salesperson approves or rejects the claim. About 99% of all claims are approved. If a claim is approved, the salesperson forwards the original claim e-mail to the accountant. If the teacher is an employee, the claim is paid in the next paycheck. Otherwise, a check is mailed to the contractor.

The Problems

The business process for handling expense claims is simple and worked when HighTree was a small company. As the volume of claims has grown, a number of problems have started happening:

- It is common for busy salespeople to miss the claim e-mails from the teachers. These e-mails get buried amid hundreds of other e-mails that each salesperson gets.
- If a salesperson goes on vacation, approval gets delayed.
- Accountants made mistakes entering claim data in the accounting system. In some cases, income tax had been deducted from the payment. (Expenses are nontaxable benefits.)
- Before a teacher can get paid, she must send in the receipts. Correlating receipts received by mail to an expense item has caused major headaches for the accountants.
- Teachers have no clear idea whether or when a claim was paid. There have been cases where unpaid expenses have gone unnoticed.

Improvement Opportunities

HighTree realizes that the expense claim process needs to be automated through a software-controlled workflow. The workflow should enter data into the accounting system. Manual data entry needs to be avoided as much as possible.

A new application needs to be developed that shows the current status of a claim. Teachers can use this software to view their claim history and make sure that they are getting paid on time.

How Can SOA Help?

As we have seen in the previous case study, SOA encourages workflow and task automation. SOA will be a perfect fit for the problems facing HighTree.

First, we need to redesign the business process. Instead of sending an e-mail, a teacher will log into a web-based application and file a claim. We will call this the *Expense Management Application* (EMA). To file a claim, a teacher needs to:

- Select the teaching assignment for which the expenses were incurred.
- Enter the total claim amount.
- Create a Microsoft Excel file containing a list of all expense items.

Once a claim is submitted, EMA issues a claim number. When the teacher mails in the receipts, this claim number is shown on the envelope.

A salesperson logs into EMA and views a list of claims that she needs to approve. Here, the business process automatically routes the claim to the correct salesperson for the teaching assignment.

If the salesperson approves the claim, the process waits for the receipts to arrive. When receipts arrive, an accountant logs into EMA, enters the claim number from the envelope, and indicates that the receipts have been received. At this point, the workflow asks the accounting system to pay the teacher (either using check or payroll).

The payment is scheduled under nontaxable benefit so that no income tax is charged.

The workflow also informs the EMA about the payment. This helps EMA show the most up-to-date status of a claim to the teachers.

Once we have optimized the business process, we need to move to the service identification stage. The players in the process are:

- **The EMA application.** The workflow informs the application as the claim goes through different stages of its lifecycle. This allows a teacher to view the latest status of a claim.
- **The accounting application.** The workflow asks this application to pay a teacher.
- **Salesperson who approves or rejects claims.** The workflow waits for a salesperson to approve or reject a claim.
- **Accountant who receives receipts sent via mail.** The workflow waits for the accountant to enter a receipt before it asks the accounting system to initiate payment.

Note that a teacher initiates the process but does not play any role within the process.

Next, we move to the service implementation phase. Exhibit 1.8 shows you how each service will be implemented.

Finally, we build the orchestration. Orchestration will automate the business process. It will ask the services to perform their tasks. Some of the tasks are long running. Usually, human tasks are like that. The orchestration can wait for certain events to take place. For example, the orchestration waits for the receipts to arrive. In short, you should be able to use orchestration to implement most common workflow scenarios.

Service Maturity and Reusability

This case study will help you understand how SOA fosters reusability. Let us have a look at the accounting system service. If we are implementing it for the first time, we will have to do the necessary work to implement the service. The same will happen if the service was already there but did not support the task of paying out nontaxable benefits.

EXHIBIT 1.8 *A list of services identified in the business process and how the services will be built*

Service	Implementation Notes
EMA	Keep in mind that EMA is a web-based application. This needs to be developed from scratch. The development of this application is outside the scope of SOA and uses traditional software development techniques such as object-oriented analysis and design (OOAD).
	However, EMA does have to implement a service. The tasks supported by this service are used by the workflow to keep the status of a claim up to date.
	EMA will implement the service as a Web Service.
Accounting System	HighTree uses a popular third-party accounting software. An external application can ask the accounting system to perform all kinds of tasks by saving a file in proprietary data format in a particular directory. One of the tasks supported by the accounting system is to add nontaxable benefit to the next payroll of an employee. Another task supports paying a contractor by check.
	In this case, we will implement the service using a file adapter. This is an example of how older software that does not offer a Web Service can still implement a service.
Salesperson	This will be a human-task service. Most SOA platform vendors allow you to develop such a service with little or no coding. The platform will also provide a web-based interface that a salesperson can use to view a list of task items (in our case, claims waiting for approval).
	Most vendors also support escalation. For example, if a salesperson is on vacation, the system will automatically move the claim to her manager's pile.
Accountant	Same as above.

We cannot avoid this upfront work, but with the SOA approach, the work can be minimal. SOA encourages us to use the functionality that is already built into the accounting software.

Over a period of time, we will keep adding more and more tasks to the service. This is called *service maturity*. As the service matures, it becomes more reusable. A new business process will most likely find that the service already supports a task that it needs.

Solution Summary

The problem involved multiple applications and people. SOA is a great methodology to solve problems like this. The problem and solution matrix in Exhibit 1.9 paints the picture.

Case Study Summary

These case studies show how the SOA approach is applied from the problem definition to the final solution. Examples are worth a thousand words. The examples here should help you understand these key points:

- SOA is a solution development approach that is ideal when the solution involves many software applications, people, machines, and business partners.

EXHIBIT 1.9 *List of problems in the case study and how they were resolved*

Problem	Solution
E-mails missed by the salesperson	The EMA software tracks the claims.
Payment delayed because salesperson is on vacation	Human-task services support escalation. If a salesperson is on vacation, her manager will approve the claim.
Accountant enters wrong data	Payment information will now be automatically entered by the orchestration as nontaxable benefit.
Major problem correlating receipts with claim	Now the receipts will be marked with the claim ID. The orchestration will use this as a correlation identifier. When receipts are entered for a claim, it will process payment for that specific claim.

- SOA takes a structured approach. First, the problems are identified. Then the business process is carefully optimized. Many of the problems are solved right at this point. Next, we identify the players or the services in the business process. Then we implement the services. Finally, we create an orchestration that automates the whole workflow.
- The line-of-business managers are actively involved in the early phases. They define the business processes and work on fixing its weaknesses. In the later phase, IT gets involved. They are responsible for implementing services and the orchestrations. SOA shines at bringing both sides to the same table. The process model and service specifications act as the common language.

NOTES

1. The SOA layers depicted in this chapter are derived in part from IBM's component layering model for SOA. For more information, check out: www.ibm.com/developerworks/webservices/library/ws-soa-design1/.
2. Emphasis added is mine. To read the full analysis from Gartner regarding SOA's long-term viability, read: Core Research Note G00144445 by Yefim V. Natis, et al.
3. Enterprise computing timeline designed by Jason Bloomberg, Copyright 2004. Used with permission.
4. René B.M. de Koster, Marisa P. de Brito, and Majsa A. van de Vendel, "How to Organise Return Handling: An Exploratory Study with Nine Retailer Warehouses," *Econometric Institute Report*, 2002, http://econpapers.repec.org/paper/dgreureir/2002264.htm.

CHAPTER 2

BUSINESS PROCESS MANAGEMENT AND SOA

Business process management (BPM) is a cornerstone of service oriented architecture (SOA). Automation of business processes is one of the key goals of SOA. BPM deals with definition and optimization of business processes. In this chapter, we explore the relationship between BPM and SOA.

WHAT IS A BUSINESS PROCESS?

Every business exists to provide some kind of value. The most common recipient of this value can be customers, partners, shareholders, and employees. The most common forms of value are goods, information, services, share price, and dividend. A business carries out a sequence of tasks to produce a specific value. This collection of tasks, their sequence, and the roles and responsibilities surrounding these tasks are collectively called a *business process*.

A business process achieves a goal that the business cares about. This is called the *output of the process*. A business process begins to execute when a certain event takes place. For example, when a customer returns a product in a retail store, the process to deal with that return begins to execute. Some of the tasks in the process may need to know certain information. For example, in the return handling process, if a task needs to increment the inventory on hand, it needs to know the SKU number of the product that has been returned. Such information is called *input to the process.*

In summary, then, these are the various components of a business process:

- **Trigger event.** This starts a business process.
- **Input to the process.** This might be information, goods, or contracts that must exist before the process can begin.
- **Tasks that need to be carried out.** The tasks can be performed by people, machine, or software. Roles and responsibilities around these tasks are well defined. Just like a process, a task can also have input and produced value (output).
- **Sequence or order of the tasks.**
- **Exception scenarios.** How does the process deal with erroneous or unusual situations?
- **Output of the process.** This is the final goal achieved by the process.

ARE YOU PROCESS ORIENTED?

Invariably, a new business or a new department starts its operations without any well-defined business processes. The activities, roles, and responsibilities are fairly unstructured. This is not because the company does not value structure and method. It is because, in the beginning, a process is not very well understood. A pattern in the day-to-day operations of the business must emerge before the processes can be defined. When you have too many exception scenarios, a pattern is hard to come by.

Once a pattern emerges that can be repeated over and over again, you are ready to start writing down the process. With business processes, the operations of a business become well defined. The quality of the output becomes consistent. Employees can be trained better. Their job becomes more streamlined and less stressful.

SOA depends heavily on business processes. Without a commitment to developing and following business processes, SOA is not likely to succeed in an organization. By the end of this chapter, the relationship between SOA and business processes should be well established.

BECOMING PROCESS ORIENTED

Building a culture of establishing and continuously fine-tuning business processes is not easy. Drawing up a process flowchart is relatively straightforward. Putting that into practice is another thing. This is especially hard in an organization that is not committed to business processes.

In an organization that is generally process oriented, a new line of business, a new partnership, or a merger can create new goals for the business. Setting up a process to achieve these goals can be equally problematic. In other words, the level of commitment of a business toward process orientation is different from the quality of a specific business process.

How does an operation go from being ad hoc and disorganized to being process oriented? It can rarely be achieved overnight. The Software Engineering Institute (SEI) of Carnegie Mellon University grappled with that issue. The output of their work is famously known as the *Capability Maturity Model Integration (CMMI)*. The model captures the way a business becomes increasingly process oriented. Although the model was originally designed for the software development industry, it is generally applicable to any business.

In CMMI, the quality of definition and management of a specific business process is called *capability*. According to the model, a process goes through five different levels of increasing capability:

> **Level 0: Incomplete or not performed.** At this very early stage, the business may be just thinking of carrying out the process. Or, the process may be performed in a partial manner.
>
> **Level 1: Performed.** At this level, employees are performing the process and achieving real goals. However, there is no management recognition of the process. There is no careful planning.

The process loosely follows a structure informally arrived at by the employees.

Level 2: Managed. At this stage, the process is carefully thought out, tuned, and well documented. Management is fully aware of it. This means that proper resources are allocated to make sure that the process completes smoothly. Roles and responsibilities are clearly laid out. Management makes sure that the employees receive training. The process is also controlled, which means that management makes sure that the employees are following the process properly.

Level 3: Defined. A defined process is a managed process that adheres to a corporate-wide standard. For example, the Asian division of a television cable company may follow a managed process to handle payment. When that process conforms to the standards followed by the divisions in the Americas and Europe, it becomes managed. Standardization should be sought only when it makes sense, keeping in mind the differences in cultural and financial landscape.

A defined process is also more rigorously described. The input and output of each task and the overall process is well understood. The roles and responsibilities of the players are well defined.

Level 4: Quantitatively managed. At this level, key performance indicators (KPIs; see later discussion) are defined and captured. The numbers are used to make sure that the business is performing at an optimal level.

Level 5: Optimizing. At this most advanced level, KPIs are used to optimize the time and cost of the process. Certain employees are made responsible for monitoring the KPIs. A system is put in place to make sure that the business is regularly looking for ways to fine-tune the process.

Before you can automate a process, it must be well understood and well defined. In the CMMI model, it should be at least in the level 2 "managed" stage.

WHAT IS BUSINESS PROCESS MANAGEMENT?

BPM is a discipline that covers all aspects of defining and performing business processes. It has the following components:

- **Define the business process.** This involves modeling the process. *Business process modeling* is a discipline in its own right, and we will discuss that in some detail in this chapter.
- **Establish the business process.** This involves activities such as training the staff and writing software to automate the tasks. This is the groundwork needed before the process is put into practice.
- **Put the process into practice and begin following the process.**
- **Monitor and control the process.** We have to make sure that everyone is following the process. Performance level of the staff is monitored and managed using the usual management practices. The time and cost performance of the business process falls directly under the jurisdiction of BPM. How long does it take from order placement to shipment? How long on average does a machine sit idle waiting for a job? How long does a part have to wait before the paint machine can process it? These numbers, if you can gather them, can indicate the vital pulse of your business. For example, a machine sitting idle for too long indicates overcapacity. A part waiting too long to get painted points to a bottleneck.
- **Improve the business process.** The urgency to fine-tune a process usually comes from the discovery that it takes too long or too much money to complete the process, that customers have shown dissatisfaction with the quality of service, or that the competition is doing things more accurately and faster. In other words, the source of pressure for continuous improvement can be either internal or external. BPM encourages an organization to form a dedicated process management team that monitors the processes, KPIs, customer satisfaction figures, and the competition, and suggests enhancements to the process.

BUSINESS PROCESS AND SOA

If, from an information technology (IT) perspective, SOA is an approach for application integration, how did business process become connected to SOA? Application integration and business process seem like the odd couple, each living in its own world. But, are they, really? By setting up a clever connection between the two, SOA opened up a slew of whole new possibilities that went beyond solving application integration problems. Let us take a moment to find out how that happened.

Conventional Enterprise Application Integration (EAI) already saw the benefit in workflow. A workflow was a sequence of nodes arranged in a flowchart-like fashion. Each node acted either as a data source or as a sink. A source contributed input data to the workflow. The workflow delivered data to the sinks. Exhibit 2.1 shows an example workflow with source and sink nodes.

In this example, customer order data is contributed by the web site. The workflow delivers the data to the accounting system and the warehouse. Obviously, all three applications use a different data format.

EXHIBIT 2.1   *In EAI, a workflow moves data from the source application to the sink applications*

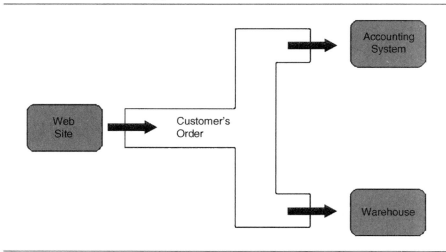

The workflow uses data conversion modules to prepare data appropriate for each sink.

The workflow approach was a great boon. It helped the EAI architects grapple with complex data synchronization problems. Individual applications no longer had to know anything about other applications' data format or programming logic. The workflow now controlled the entire flow path of the data from a central location. We can use an example to illustrate that point. In the workflow as shown in Exhibit 2.1, data is being delivered simultaneously to the accounting and warehouse systems. If, for some reason, the accounting system must complete processing the order before it can be sent to the warehouse, we can easily change the workflow to reflect that. This is shown in Exhibit 2.2.

SOA took workflow to its next level—a business process. Look at the workflow diagram in Exhibit 2.2 again. We know that customer's order data is getting copied to the accounting system and the warehouse. But, what are the sinks doing with the data? Are we processing a new order? Or, is this an update to an order that has been already placed? Is the accounting system checking for credit? Or, is it preparing an invoice? We cannot tell.

What if we could replace the data sources and sinks with tasks and activities? Exhibit 2.3 shows how the workflow can be converted to a business process.

EXHIBIT **2.2** *A workflow can be easily altered to change the flow of information*

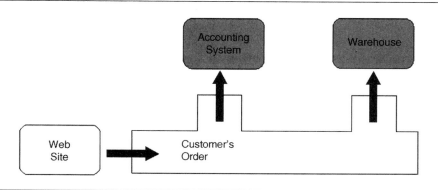

EXHIBIT **2.3**   *Business process example*

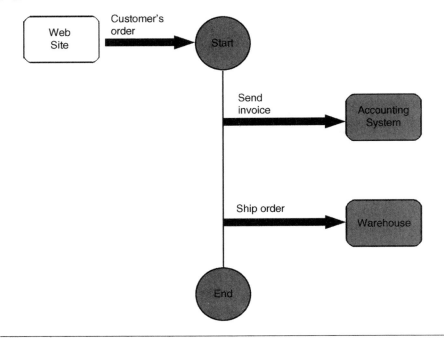

The workflow now has become a sequence of activities—in other words, a business process. The roles of each application in this integrated solution becomes clear. The web site is acting as the data source since it supplies the customer order data to the business process. Placement of an order on the web site acts as a trigger and the business process is initiated. The business process asks the accounting system to send the invoice. The order data is sent as input to that request. Similarly, the business process asks the warehouse system to ship the order.

The change was almost subtle. SOA replaced the IT centric notions such as data source and sink with management centric objects like tasks, roles, and responsibilities. SOA also does not mandate that these tasks be performed entirely by software. They can be performed by people, software, and by external organizations. In case of the last one, the exact nature of how a task is carried out may be completely opaque to the organization that owns and executes the process. SOA really confronts IT to think beyond software and understand how the business operates where not everything can be automated through software.

ALIGNING IT WITH THE BUSINESS

The business leaders have been spending considerable energy toward business process optimization. IT had been spending a great deal of their time and money building application integration solutions. The world of the two remained disconnected.

When SOA proposed using business process for application integration, a bridge was formed between the two. Both can now come to the table, have the same goal, and speak the same language. The common goal is the definition and smooth execution of the business processes in a way that best meets the company's targets and customer's expectations.

BECOMING SERVICE ORIENTED

All businesses are inherently service oriented. Employees offer services by performing certain tasks. Machines manufacture goods. Software applications store and offer information. The organization as a whole provides certain services to its customers and partners.

When IT recognizes this pattern and adopts service as the foundation of everything a company does, it becomes service oriented. SOA, then, encourages a business to be process oriented and IT to be service oriented.

What, then, is the relationship between business process and service? A business process is a sequence of activities. Employees, machines, and software systems perform these activities. They are called *service providers*, or, in short, *services*. Each service is capable of performing a few tasks. A business process acts as a conductor in an orchestra and asks the service providers to perform specific tasks. And in this way, services become the building blocks of a business.

In SOA, a business process literally runs as software. This is known as *business process automation*. An automated business process is also known as *orchestration*. Essentially, the orchestration software does the coordination of tasks that eventually complete a business goal. For the first time, key business operations are overseen, controlled, and managed by a piece of software. Even the most complex operations, involving suppliers, partners, government, human beings, and software, can be coordinated in this way. This phenomenon can be compared with the Airbus 320, which was the first major airplane to be piloted by software. A note of caution, however. Leaving the day to day supervision of a process to an orchestration software will require a lot of trust from the managers. The process has to be very mature and well understood for you to be able to build all possible eventualities in to the orchestration. On the positive side, managers will get involved with supervision only if an unforeseen scenario occurs. This will free up time for them to focus more on the time, cost, and customer-satisfaction performance of the process.

It is tempting to think that automating a process will improve its performance. But that is not true. A poorly designed process that takes too long and costs too much will continue to be that way after you have automated it. SOA does not magically make a process more efficient. It does provide ways which, when used, can improve a process. For example, you can eliminate duplicate manual data entry in multiple systems by having the orchestration automatically transfer the data to these systems.

FROM OBJECT TO SERVICE ORIENTATION

For the technical executives, the parallel between service orientation and object orientation is unmistakable. Principles such as abstraction and generalization already exist in the real world. When IT begins to model software artifacts that follow these principles, it becomes object oriented.

IT does not make a business object or service oriented. Instead, it orients its own practices for modeling and developing software by adopting the principles of the real world.

Object oriented analysis and design (OOAD) had tremendous impact on IT. Business problems were captured as use cases. They were then analyzed to define classes, such as Customer and Order. The approach allowed IT to grapple with complex problems. A software application developed using this approach is generally easier to understand and maintain.

As successful as OOAD was, its scope was limited to individual software applications. Objects were the building blocks of a single application. Unfortunately, a business rarely does anything using just one software application, or using just software, for that matter.

So, we needed a new software development methodology that looked at the bigger picture of the products of a business and how it goes about producing them. That means, within the boundary of the business it needed to consider all available resources—personnel, machines, and software—as contributors to production. Outside the boundary of the business it needed to look at how the organization interacts with its customers, government bodies, suppliers, and partners. And thus, SOA was born.

BUSINESS PROCESS MODELING

The main goal of process modeling is to formally define and document a business process. When the pattern of activities in a process has become repeatable and well understood, you are ready to define the process.

The discipline of process modeling goes beyond just process definition. You can optimize a process *before* it is put into practice. A process model can also help you plan for workforce and materiel and budget for expenses.

Business analysts (BAs) perform business process modeling. They work very closely with the line of business managers who are directly responsible for the efficiency and profitability of a division (also known as the stakeholders). In object-oriented development, the role of the business managers was minimal. BAs interviewed the stakeholders to elicit the requirements. The business managers rarely reviewed the deliverables of the BA (class diagrams, etc.). The situation could not be any more different in SOA. BAs learn the existing structure of the process by interviewing the managers. Any changes to the process must be reviewed and approved by the managers. In most cases, the ideas for process improvement will come from the business managers. In fact, we expect and encourage the line of business managers to learn the tools of process modeling and get directly involved in the modeling activities.

Choosing a Modeling Tool

In its simplest form, you can model a process as a plain-text document, a hand-drawn flowchart, or a Visio™ diagram. More advanced tools will help you in optimizing a process and resource planning.

When choosing a modeling tool, we recommended that you look at the features shown in Exhibit 2.4. Calculate the total score for each modeling tool under consideration. The final score will give you some idea for the comprehensive capability of the tool.

We will now go through the various stages of process modeling.

Define the As-Is Process

Process definition describes the sequence of tasks in a process. *As-is* represents the current understanding of the process. Even though you may mean to improve on the current process, it is recommended that you start by modeling the process as it stands right now. This will help you compare the performance of the new and improved version of the process with the current process. We will discuss this shortly.

The process is drawn in a flowchart-like diagram. The diagram is made up of various building blocks or *nodes*. The nodes can be divided into three main categories:

1. **Activity.** These are tasks performed by various service providers. (See Exhibit 2.5 for examples of activity nodes.)

EXHIBIT **2.4** *Important features in a business process modeling tool*

Feature	Why Important?	Importance Level 1 = Nice to have 5 = Very important
Supports common modeling notations (start, stop, activity, conditional logic, parallel paths, loops)	These are the basic building blocks of a business process.	5
Supports advanced notations (subprocess, timer)	These notations are important for modeling complex processes. But, not all SOA platforms may support them.	3
Can import and export BPEL (Business Process Execution Language) document	In SOA, BPEL is the most popular and preferred file format to capture the definition of a business process.	5
	Not all SOA platforms work with BPEL for process definition. If your SOA vendor uses a proprietary format, make sure that the modeling tool can export the process definition in that format.	
Allows you to define KPIs	KPIs are essential for monitoring the performance of a process.	4
Allows you to allocate resources for the activities	Resource allocation will help you estimate the resource demand and cost of a process.	3
Can execute a process in a simulated environment	Simulation allows you to see how the process will perform before it is actually put into practice.	3
Export simulation result report	You should be able to create a report that shows the estimated cost and duration for running the process. This will help you explain the optimizations to the stakeholders.	2

EXHIBIT **2.5**   *Commonly used activity nodes*

Type	Description
Receive	A process receives input data using this node. The receive node is connected to a trigger event. When the event occurs, a new instance of the business process is started.
Reply	This node is used to return information to whatever started the process. Information can be only a part of the output produced by a process. Other outputs include goods manufactured and orders shipped.
Invoke	One of the most important nodes, the Invoke activity asks a service provider to perform a task. For example, a manager can be asked to approve an expense claimed by an employee.

2. **Flow control.** Nodes like conditional logic and loop fall in this category. (See Exhibit 2.6 for examples of flow control nodes.)
3. **Error handling.** These nodes help you model the exception situations. (See Exhibit 2.7 for examples of error-handling nodes.)

An example of a business process model will be useful at this point. In case study B: Expense Claim, we introduced the expense claim process. Exhibit 2.8 shows the model for this process.

In this model, the claim record is received by the ReceiveClaim activity. A new instance of the process is started to deal with that claim (each claim starts a new instance). The ApproveClaim is an Invoke activity (refer to Exhibit 2.5 for the shape of the icon of an Invoke activity). It asks the employee's manager to approve or reject the claim.

The ClaimApproved Switch node then takes a different set of actions based on the outcome of the manager's decision. If the claim is approved, the claim is marked as approved. The employee is then notified. The process then asks the accounting system to pay the employee in the next paycheck. If, however, the claim is denied, no payment is made.

EXHIBIT **2.6** *Commonly used flow-control nodes*

Type	Description
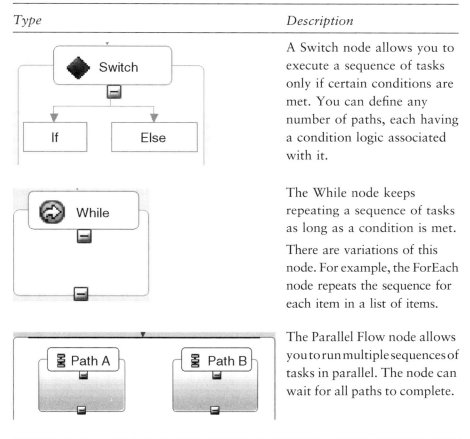	A Switch node allows you to execute a sequence of tasks only if certain conditions are met. You can define any number of paths, each having a condition logic associated with it.
	The While node keeps repeating a sequence of tasks as long as a condition is met. There are variations of this node. For example, the ForEach node repeats the sequence for each item in a list of items.
	The Parallel Flow node allows you to run multiple sequences of tasks in parallel. The node can wait for all paths to complete.

Allocate Resources and Time for the Activities

A key part of BPM is continuous improvement of a process. Let us say that you as a business analyst want to make a few changes to a process, hoping that they will reduce the demand for resources and consequently cut cost. You need to be fairly certain that the changes will have the desired impact before you put those changes into effect. Changing a process is not always trivial for a business. The line of business managers might not even see eye-to-eye with you and disapprove the changes.

What you need is a proof-of-concept environment where you can try out the process. This is obviously not practical in real life. You cannot

EXHIBIT 2.7   *Commonly used error-handling nodes*

Type	Description
Exit	This node, when executed, terminates the process instance.
Throw	If the process runs into an exception condition, it can raise an error. The error can then be handled from within the process or by the entity that started the process.
Compensate	The Compensate node is used to ask the process engine to start undoing the work done by the activities that had already finished doing their work.

simply have part of the business carry out the unproven version of the business process. Business process simulation is the solution to this problem. Simulation allows you to run the process in a software environment. If you have configured the resource usage, duration, and cost of completing each task, simulation can fairly accurately predict the performance of a process. You also will be able to locate hidden problems in the process. We will cover simulation in more detail shortly. For now, we have to get the process model ready for it.

First, define the types of resources that complete various tasks in a process. For example, Quality Assurance Staff, Trucks, Machines. You can leave out Software Application as a resource, because typically they cost very little to complete an operation.

For each resource type, specify:

- Name of the resource expressed in terms of the role it plays (such as Quality Assurance Staff and not Billy Bob).
- Skills and capabilities expected from the resource. This will help you communicate the resource requirements to the line of business managers and eventually to the human resources department.
- Hourly wage, rental, or running cost.

EXHIBIT **2.8**   *Model for the expense claim process*

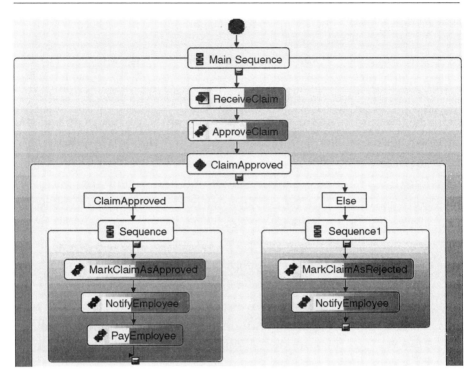

- Per-process cost. For example, moving trucks may charge for the time it takes to travel to a location.

Then, for each activity in the process, specify:

- Resource types that perform the task.
- Quantity of resources for each type.
- Time spent before the task can even begin. This is the preparation time.
- Time it takes to complete the task. To keep things simple, we can assume all resources are occupied while the task is in progress.

It may be difficult to come up with a precise duration for the tasks. A good modeling tool will let you specify a ballpark figure using a probability distribution model.

We are now ready to move to the simulation phase.

Run Simulation

A few things need to be set up before we can let the process run:

- The frequency of the trigger event that starts the process. For example, if a process starts every time an insurance claim is made, you need to specify the frequency of claims. The frequency may be different at different times of day. It can be different during the weekends. A good modeling tool will help you capture these subtleties.
- For each resource type, you need to tell the system how many resources you have on hand. Resource content happens when trigger events are firing and new process instances are starting at a rapid rate and you do not have enough resources to get involved in all process instances. For example, at around 11 A.M., you may have 134 insurance claims filed over the phone. If you have only 35 insurance adjusters, some of the process instances will have to wait.

    Alternatively, you can say that you have an unlimited number of resources. When the simulation is run, none of the process instances will have to wait to procure enough resources. This will help you to determine the peak demand for resources. In the previous example, if every insurance claim needs to be looked at by an adjuster, you will need approximately 134 of them. This type of analysis is great when you have a budget available to procure more resources but you are not sure how much of which resources you need.
- How long will the simulation run? You can set the value in hours, days, or weeks. The tool will actually compress time. For example, it will start a day's worth of process instances in a few seconds. It will proportionately scale down the duration for the activities. You should run the simulation long enough to get enough sample data.

After the simulation run ends, you will be able to view a number of result data items. The most important ones are shown in Exhibit 2.9.

EXHIBIT **2.9**   *Typical metrics gathered from a simulation run*

Result Data	Meaning
Average process duration	A good estimate of how long the process will take from start to finish. A faster process invariably leads to lower cost and better customer satisfaction.
Average cost per process instance	This is the sum total of the cost of every activity in a process. Note that not all activities are always executed. For example, for minor claims an adjuster does not have to get involved. In your process model, you should be able to define the probability of each condition happening in real life.
For each activity, the average time spent waiting for resources	Waiting happens due to resource contention. This number is a great way to pinpoint bottlenecks in the process. You can effectively increase resources in the right area to eliminate the bottleneck.
	The number can also indicate customers' average waiting time.
For each activity, the peak number of process instances that had to wait for resources	This can indicate the size of the lineup. For example, in a grocery store checkout process, if you see that 15 process instances were waiting to clear the checkout activity, you have about 15 customers waiting in the lineup.
Total yearly wage	For each resource type, the system can calculate the total cost and extrapolate that for the whole year. This helps you achieve accurate budgeting.

Model the To-Be Process

The *to-be* process is an improvement of the as-is process. Basic goals of improvement are:

- Lower the cost of doing business.
- Lower the resource demand.

- Reduce the time it takes to complete the process.
- Reduce customer wait times.
- Reduce customer lineup size.

All of these goals are highly interrelated.

BPM spends much energy on the principles of process optimization. We will not get into the details here.

Measure the Difference

Run simulations of the to-be process with the exact same parameters (resource pool size, trigger frequency, etc.) as you used for the as-is process. Then compare the key result data with the data from the two processes. This will quantitatively show the effect the changes had. Based on this analysis, if needed, make more changes to the to-be process until you see a definite improvement.

Export a summary report that compares the key result data for the two processes. Show this report to the line of business managers to win their approval of the to-be process.

It is worth noting that business process modeling is a mini-version of BPM. Both look at key performance data and find ways to tune the process. However, during business process modeling, we rely on simulated result data; in contrast, BPM looks at real-life data. We will cover this live monitoring of processes shortly.

ESTABLISH THE BUSINESS PROCESS

Getting ready to put a new process into motion requires administrative activities such as employee training, resource procurement, and signing of contracts. SOA does not change that. Consequently, we will not get into the details in this book.

SOA, however, requires that a software component be created that will control the flow of activities in a process. This software artifact is popularly called *process orchestration, process choreographer*, or just plain *business process*.

The idea of a software-based orchestration system must have been influenced by the assembly-line concept used so effectively by the manufacturing industry. In an assembly line, the work product moves from one work area to the next. In each work area, a machine or human workers perform a specific task. The concerns and responsibilities of the service providers in each work area are completely isolated from the rest of the work areas. This separation of concerns allows workers to do one thing and do it with exceptional accuracy and efficiency.

In SOA, the orchestration keeps things moving. It decides what task should be performed at any given point of time. Services perform these tasks. Services are fairly isolated from each other and in most cases do not even know of each other's existence.

IT is responsible for developing the process orchestration. It will do that by closely following the process delivered to it by the business analysts. You want to make this handoff process as smooth as possible. Ideally, you want the process modeling tool to export the model in a format that the developers can easily import into their tool. Most SOA vendors have adopted a standard way for the developers to define the orchestration. This standard is known as *Business Process Execution Language (BPEL)*.

IT also has to develop the services. It does so by following a structured methodology called *service oriented analysis and design (SOAD)*. SOAD is a still-emerging discipline and well beyond the scope of this book. You should, however, take the time to learn more about what a service looks like.

Nature of a Service

The tasks in a business process are performed by various services. A service has three main components:

1. **Service interface.** This describes the tasks a service is capable of performing.
2. **Service implementation.** This is a specific service provider, such as your SAP system or Bob in the human resources department.

3. **Service endpoint.** *Endpoint* refers to where the service can be found (its address).

Splitting a service into these three distinct parts has many business advantages. First, the service interface is merely a collection of operations or tasks. It does not concern itself about who is going to do these tasks. Anyone who needs these tasks to be done is called a *service consumer.* An orchestration is a famous consumer because it asks the service to carry out certain tasks. In SOA, a consumer should not directly know about a service provider. Instead it should work with a service interface. For example, in our expense claim handling process, the orchestration needs to ask the accounting software to pay the employee. The orchestration should ask an abstract and generic accounting system to perform the task. It should not directly know about the make, model, and vendor of the accounting system. That part is taken care of by the service implementation.

A service may be implemented by a software application, a human being, a machine, or another organization. The exact nature of the service is hidden from the consumer (Exhibit 2.10). This is called *loose coupling* between the consumer and the provider. There are several advantages to this. In the context of our expense claim process, these could be the benefits:

- Currently, you may be using Oracle Financial as the accounting software. If your organization gets acquired and the accounting

EXHIBIT **2.10** *Multiple service providers can follow the same service interface. To a consumer, all providers appear the same and they are interchangeable*

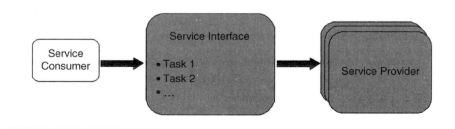

system changes to J.D. Edwards, the expense claim business process does not have to change. Conceptually, the process needs to ask the accounting system to pay the employee, irrespective of who the vendor of the accounting system is.

- A human user will most likely offer the ApproveClaim task. If the volume of expense claims gets to be very high, you may want to automatically approve some of the low-value claims. The implementation of this service can be changed from a purely human service to a mix of software and human service. Once again, the main business process does not have to change.

MONITOR AND CONTROL THE PROCESS

With an orchestration your business process runs on autopilot. If everything goes according to plan, all the tasks in a process will complete successfully and in time. The sequencing of tasks no longer needs any human supervision. The role of human staff is largely limited to performing the tasks (but not to control the flow or sequence of these tasks).

Unfortunately, we cannot take our eyes completely off the business process. There are several things that can go wrong:

- **A task has not finished in time.** This may be because an employee is on vacation, a supplier is really not up to the game, or someone just forgot all about it. Something has to be done to deal with this situation so that the assembly line of the business process can get moving. Even the simplest of tasks can unnecessarily hold up a process.
- **Process instances are starting at an alarming rate, increasing demand for resources.** For example, in our Return Handling case study, you may see a high number of returns after the holiday period. Excessive demand for resources can lead to long customer lines, overflow in a storage area, and in a worst-case scenario, machine failure.

- **An unexpected situation has occurred.** For example, a supplier has sent a wrong part. The business process is not designed to deal with that situation. Something has to be done to reorder the part so that the manufacturing process can continue. If an exception situation occurs, management should consider altering the process to deal with it. Manual intervention to resolve a problem can slow down a process.
- **An error has occurred.** For example, a software application had crashed and the orchestration could not contact it. IT should try to design the system to be as fault tolerant as possible. However, not all possible error conditions can be automatically rectified. In some cases, human intervention will be needed.

This is why we need to constantly monitor the process instances. Even small problems, if left unattended, lead to major issues. Proper monitoring helps you address problems more proactively. This is one of the greatest advantages of running a business process using orchestration software.

There are two ways to monitor the process:

1. **Using alerts.** In this approach, you can configure the maximum time limit for the activities. If an activity takes longer than the limit, an e-mail or SMS (Short Message Service) message can be sent to a manager. The same can be done for the unexpected and error situations.
2. **Using periodic reporting.** In this approach, someone periodically pulls up a report of process instances that are held up for too long or have failed due to an error.

Monitoring will help you to detect problems but not to deal with them. Resolving problems in a business process is a complicated matter. Below are a few commonly used techniques to deal with error situations:

- If a task had failed, locate and fix the reason behind the failure. Retry the task and let the process continue.

- Simply terminate the process and start from beginning. This can work only if the half-finished task did not leave any lingering effect.
- Undo the work already done by the tasks. Then terminate the process. Work is undone by a reverse process called *compensation flow*.

If monitoring is used to detect problems, controlling is used to improve the overall performance of the process. As the process instances start and finish, the system keeps track of important statistics, known as the *key performance indicators (KPIs)*. A KPI stands for a measurable objective of the business. KPI is a very broad topic and encompasses all aspects of a business. A few example KPIs are shown below:

- Sales objectives, such as profit and revenue target.
- Trend. What are the highest selling products? What geographical regions are experiencing the highest growth? In our Return Handling case study, we would like to know about the products that have the highest likelihood of being returned.
- Operational efficiency. These KPI metrics deal with the time and cost performance of various tasks and entire business processes. For example, how long does it take on average to touch up a returned product? How long does an employee wait to get paid for an expense claim?
- Customer and employee satisfaction levels.

In BPM, you need to decide what metrics are relevant for a business process. For each metric, you need to have a target value and a boundary limit indicating the worst-case scenario. On a day-to-day basis, if a KPI metric falls below the limit, an alarm should be raised so that someone can address the problem right away. We have already discussed this as a part of process monitoring. Every few weeks, business managers need to review the KPI values to make sure that the business is meeting its targets. If the targets are consistently missed, either there is a very high expectation or there is something wrong with the process design.

How can you gather the KPI values? There are a few ways:

- Financial figures such as revenue and profit can be obtained from the accounting software.
- Trend data is produced by the data warehousing and business intelligence software.
- Customer and employee satisfaction levels are gauged by surveys and focus groups.
- Operational efficiency metrics can be gathered by the SOA platform that executes the business process orchestration. Essentially, here is where SOA and BPM contribute to KPI gathering and analysis. KPIs are defined as a part of the process model. As the process instances run, you can view the live data in a dashboard. You can also view summary reports for a range of time periods.

IMPROVE OR ALTER THE BUSINESS PROCESS

Continuous improvement of operational efficiency is a key goal of BPM. The motivation to make changes to a process can come from suboptimal KPI values, changing business conditions (new partnerships or new customers), changes to government regulations, and pressure from the competition. Details of process optimization are beyond the scope of this book. We should, however, discuss how SOA helps the reengineering activity.

SOA is supposed make a business more agile. By that we mean that a business can implement a change to its processes faster once the need for the change is realized. Exactly how does SOA do that?

The factors that take up the time between the remodeling of a process and putting the process into practice include retraining of staff, informing the partner and supplier, and finally, writing new software. SOA shortens the time IT takes to implement the necessary changes. SOA does this by following two principles: *service reuse* and *service abstraction*.

How Does Service Reuse Help?

Recall from our earlier discussions that an orchestration asks various services to perform certain tasks. As long as the modified process does not call for a brand-new task to be carried out, we can simply use the existing services to implement the orchestration. That means that the new process model is free to do things in a different order, or do various things in parallel, and none of these changes will require IT to build new services.

In the beginning, the number of services and the kinds of tasks they can perform will be small. In many cases, a new or modified process will need to do an activity that no existing service can perform. The level of reuse will be low at this point. As the services become more mature, you will begin to see more reuse. With fewer services to develop, IT will be able to turn around and complete a change much faster. This is shown in Exhibit 2.11.

EXHIBIT **2.11** *Graph showing service maturity and decreasing IT turnaround time*

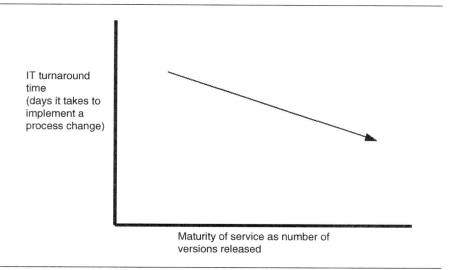

IT turnaround time (days it takes to implement a process change)

Maturity of service as number of versions released

How Does Service Abstraction Help?

We have already discussed how an orchestration should work with a generic or abstract representation of a service. This service is then connected to a real service provider. Let us say that you have a new parts supplier. The abstract service can be connected to a new service developed for this supplier. This way, we do spend the time to develop the new service, but we do not change the orchestration in any way. Also, if you have a slew of processes that manage the interaction with the suppliers (price quote, ordering, order status checking, etc.), all of them could start using the new partner's service without much additional development work.

Generally speaking, abstraction helps you when you have identified a pattern among the various service providers who provide similar types of services. An abstract or generic representation of a service acts like a broker between the business process and the actual service provider. This shields the business process from the actual service provider. You can easily integrate new service providers or replace one with another. Examples of abstract services could be Supplier, Manufacturer, Accounting System, and Warehouse System. The following are a few example cases where abstraction pays off:

- Your company has acquired a small company. Expenses claimed by the employees of this company need to be paid out by the accounting system of that company, at least for a while until the new company is fully integrated with yours. Here, we can define an abstract service called Accounting System. The accounting systems of the parent and newly acquired companies are the actual service providers.

- The call center of your company has been outsourced to an overseas company. The return handling process now has to interact with the new call center application. Abstract service: Call Center. Here, abstraction helps us replace a service provider without having to change the business processes.

- Your company needs to lease space from a warehouse. This warehouse uses an application that is different from the application your own warehouses use. Abstract service: Warehouse System. Here, abstraction helps us integrate a new service provider into the organization.

SUMMARY

If you are new to BPM, this chapter should have given you a gentle introduction to the discipline. More important, the purpose of this chapter is to show the relationship between BPM and SOA. We went through the full life cycle of BPM, from modeling to process reengineering, and saw how the BPM and SOA principles working together create new value for the business.

CHAPTER 3

SOA VALUE PROPOSITION

By now you likely have some insight into the potential value that service orientation holds for your enterprise. The question remains, What is the real driving motivation behind service orientation? With so much hype and energy around service oriented architecture (SOA), it is tempting to think that service orientation is the right answer for every business or for every situation. Common sense and practical experience indicate otherwise. This chapter delves into the value-add associated with service orientation.

SOA VALUE STORY

Ronald Schmelzer, of industry think tank ZapThink, describes four key benefits to SOA:[1] (1) reducing integration expenses (both development costs and maintenance costs), (2) increasing asset reuse (no need to reinvent the wheel each time), (3) increasing business agility (the pace of business has changed, but few enterprises have), and (4) reducing business risk (both operational and compliance risk). In the following sections, we will explore and illustrate each of these value propositions.

Reducing Integration Expenses

> If I had a dollar for every time that upper management asked me to cut costs . . .   —A CTO who is fond of *irony*

Cost cutting is a common demand that is levied on technology organizations. Consequently, each new paradigm within the industry (e.g., client-server, Web/*n*-tier, SOA, etc.) is pitched by some as a cost-cutting strategy. The trouble is that many enterprises attempt some grand enterprise-wide deployment rather than incrementally growing their SOA over time and incorporating lessons learned along the way. The fact is that, if properly implemented, SOA actually can reduce both development and maintenance costs. Use of loosely coupled, standards-based interfaces keeps integration costs low. By leveraging standard protocols, data formats, and interfaces, a great deal of traditional integration costs can be mitigated or even entirely avoided. Additionally, SOA's push toward loosely coupled system integration allows for a reduction in time spent writing and ultimately maintaining custom integration logic. Some enterprises even see a reduction in middleware maintenance licensing fees by moving to standard Web Services interfaces rather than paying for a large stack of licenses in order to connect systems via various proprietary connectors and adapters.

Another way that SOA helps to keep costs low is by reducing the impact of making significant system and infrastructure changes. The multiple levels of granularity within SOA (recall the SOA stack examined in Chapter 1) facilitate changes to business processes and system use cases while minimizing the impact to the software baseline.

SOA reduces system maintenance and development costs associated with the deployment of new solutions by isolating components and systems through well-defined interfaces and proper architectural layering. To understand this better, consider Exhibit 3.1. In a standard enterprise environment, integration points between systems are tightly coupled:

- Vendor, platform, and/or language-specific bindings.
- Application-specific data formats are used.
- Application-specific application provider interfaces (APIs) are directly leveraged.

Each system in Exhibit 3.1 is directly connected to the systems with which it must interact during the course of operation. In some cases,

EXHIBIT **3.1** *Tightly integrated enterprise environment*

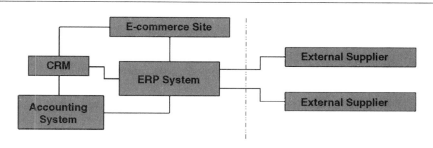

external partners are even coming in through the firewall to directly access enterprise systems. In this particular example, the enterprise resource planning (ERP) system is a key component of the enterprise (typical for manufacturing, engineering, and product-centric businesses). It is a mission-critical system that the entire supply chain hinges upon. When significant changes need to be made to such a system (either upgrading to a new system or even just moving to the next major release), the impact of such a change can ripple throughout the enterprise. Exhibit 3.2 illustrates this ripple-effect, impacting other systems and even the external systems of external business partners.

So how does SOA help with this? If you remember the SOA stack introduced in Chapter 1, these layers of abstraction insulate the enterprise so that changes do not ripple past interface boundaries. By containing the impact of these changes, service orientation keeps development and

EXHIBIT **3.2** *Changes to the tightly integrated environment produce a catastrophic ripple effect*

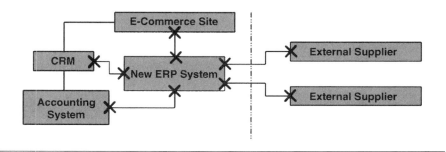

maintenance costs low and also reduces risk (another value proposition that we will discuss in the "Reducing Risk" section).

Increasing Asset Reuse

Question: What do the following things have in common?
- Disposable diapers
- Paper plates
- Air filters
- Application software

Answer: None of them have ever been designed to be reused.

While some might take exception to this, the reality is that *reuse* has become something of a holy grail in the information technology (IT) realm. Project managers, business divisions, and even entire enterprises have been chasing it for decades and many have concluded that it is merely a well-fabricated myth. It should come as no surprise, then, that proponents of service orientation are heralding the value of reuse as a major reason to adopt SOA. Those who are relatively new to the industry are quite excited about the prospects of service oriented reuse. Those of us who have been around for a while, however, recognize that each new technology wave takes up the reuse mantra and espouses the virtues of its particular approach. Service orientation falls prey to this as well. In an attempt to determine the validity of SOA's reuse claim, we will start by examining software reuse in general; then we will highlight the shortcomings of previous strategies, and finally examine the potential for SOA to actually deliver on the promise of reuse.

Copy-and-Paste as Reuse

Reuse has been tried before. We have tried reusing subroutines, functions, objects, and, eventually, components. Each time we have suffered from one fundamental weakness. No matter how clever the reuse strategy was from a software development standpoint, once we moved into production we had to deploy the software as a local module or library

EXHIBIT **3.3** *Traditional reuse is more like glorified copy-and-paste*

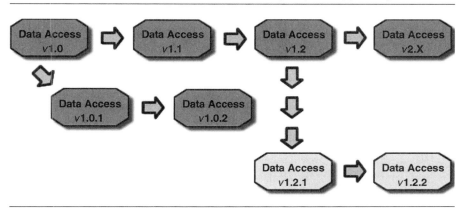

for each system that needs that capability. For example, one team develops a software library for data access. Another team needs the same capability, so they get a copy of that library and deploy it on their server. Then the first team upgrades to the next version. Then a third project borrows the library and modifies it for their needs for a different application. Before long, there are three or four variations running around, no central version of the truth, and no way to provide direct access to a common library at runtime (see Exhibit 3.3). Every time someone wants to "reuse" this data library, another copy is placed out onto a server and the potential for another development branch is created. So, in theory we have reuse. In practice, it is just glorified copy-and-paste.

Service Oriented Reuse

Reusing services is a bit different. A service is created and hosted in one place. If another application or system needs to utilize that service, it simply needs to send an appropriately formatted message to the service address (see Exhibit 3.4). Additional copies of the service do not get distributed all over the enterprise. Certainly there still will be a need for additional versions of the service to be created, but they are centrally managed and additional uses of the service can be easily supported without losing control.

EXHIBIT 3.4 *Service oriented reuse enables capabilities to be reused in different contexts*

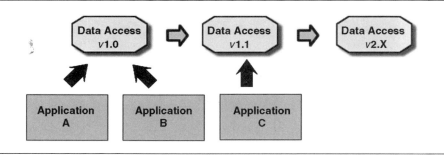

Increasing Agility

There was a time in the not-too-distant past when the pace of business was a bit slower than it is today. You could leave a message for someone and not expect a response for days, and deploy new products and solutions in months or years rather than days or weeks. If a company had a bad quarter, the market was forgiving and the prevailing mentality was to wait and see how the company performs the remainder of the year. Fast-forward to modern days and you are thrust into a 24/7 business cycle. Messages must be returned the same day, new products and services developed in a matter of weeks, and if a company's stock is tanking in the morning, investors are questioning the chief executive officer's (CEO's) grip on business by lunchtime. Customers and the market at large seem to value speed and responsiveness over safe, methodical business practices. Responding to opportunities in a matter of weeks or months is no longer acceptable. Previously, this was the advantage of working with smaller firms, but now even large organizations are expected to be nimble and able to adapt quickly to new opportunities. This is what is meant by the term *agility*. Agility is a measure of how quickly an organization can modify existing capabilities, create new products and services, or modify business processes. Service orientation raises the visibility of underlying business rules and enables rapid turnaround of new and modified business capabilities. By breaking monolithic information systems into a collection of services, business capabilities can be more quickly and easily modified. For example, a company might have developed some customer account profile services and order-tracking services for use internally by employees. Later, there is a desire to create a customer account management portal to serve customers better and reduce the number of calls made to the customer support center. As illustrated in Exhibit 3.5, the existing services could be used to provide access to customer profile and order history and a few additional services created to add visibility into the technical support database. All of these services could be consumed by a Web portal that is then made available to customers. In the absence of an SOA, all of these capabilities would need to be built from scratch or, at a minimum, copied from other applications and then integrated into the new application. Either way, a service oriented solution is faster and cheaper to develop. That is how SOA enables agile business.

EXHIBIT **3.5**   *Service orientation enables business agility*

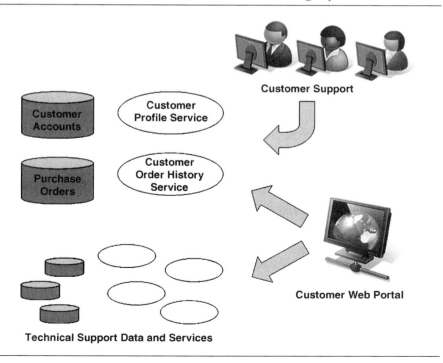

Reducing Risk

As the old saying goes, "Never be afraid to try something new; amateurs built the Ark; professionals built the Titanic." Although everyone recognizes the value of taking risks from time to time, effective risk management is a crucial element to successful business practices. Service orientation reduces two categories of risk: operational risk and compliance risk.

SOA Reduces Operational Risk

By breaking system functionality into discrete services, SOA requires teams to touch fewer components in order to develop new capabilities as well as make changes to existing ones, thus lowering risk. Additionally, service layering (as discussed and illustrated in Chapter 1) allows testing to be isolated and focused on only the changed processes and/or services. Well-defined interfaces, modular services, and distinct enterprise layers all work together to produce an environment with lower operational risks. Exhibit 3.6 illustrates how a service oriented

EXHIBIT 3.6   *The use of a business process and data map illustrates how SOA reduces operational risk*

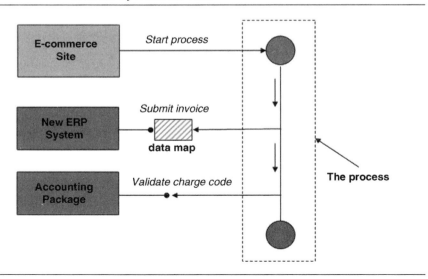

enterprise architecture can help to insulate a business from even major system changes such as introducing a new system into an existing business process flow. Through well-defined interfaces and data mapping, SOA can accommodate a significant change while minimizing the impact to existing business processes.

SOA Reduces Compliance Risk

Service orientation also reduces the risk to which organizations in regulatory environments are exposed. Regulatory compliance is made more manageable due to the agility afforded by SOA. Regulations like the Sarbanes-Oxley Act (SOX), Health Insurance Portability and Accountability Act (HIPAA), USA PATRIOT Act, and others are inherently arbitrary and subject to change based on political pressure and societal priorities. SOA supports quick and complete compliance with changing legislation through a process-centric, layered system design. Regulatory compliance is a complex, and ever-evolving animal. Compliance requirements can change based on political pressure, world events, or the natural evolution of legislation. For example, although HIPAA was passed in the United States in 1996, new regulations ("rules") continue to be released. In 2006, the "Unique Identifiers Rule" went into effect, requiring the use of a new National Provider Identifier (NPI) as a unique identifier for electronic communications used by health plans and all government programs (Medicare, Medicaid, etc.). Traditionally, enterprises would have needed to update their data tables, reporting tools, and application business logic. A process-centric SOA offers a much more elegant solution, however. As Exhibit 3.7 illustrates, a service is introduced into all affected business processes to perform a mapping between NPIs and the internal identifiers expected by the enterprise's information systems. Not only does this result in quick and complete compliance, but it has the added benefit that it can be modified, removed, or otherwise replaced in the future when the rules regarding provider identifiers change again!

EXHIBIT **3.7** *A business process in concert with a well-defined service illustrates how SOA reduces compliance risk*

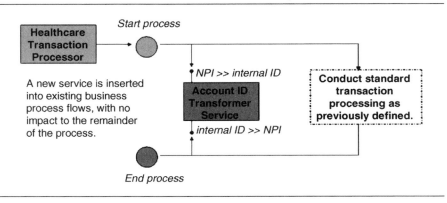

SOA VALUE, BEYOND THE CORE

Thus far we have looked at several valid reasons to adopt SOA: reducing integration expenses, increasing asset reuse, business agility, and reducing risk. There are additional value propositions for service orientation that are beginning to emerge within organizations, such as alignment, time-to-market, visibility, and modernization.

Alignment

Business process management (BPM) efforts have attempted to align technology teams with business strategy via well-defined business process workflows. While BPM had some success with refining and aligning human processes, technology assets proved not to be nearly as malleable. Information systems were developed as tightly integrated silos with embedded business logic. Adaptability was not a part of the design. SOA changes this. SOA breaks technology silos and monoliths into configurable services with well-defined interfaces that are ripe for inclusion into a dynamic business process that is aligned with business strategy. The synergy between SOA and BPM is tremendous, leading some organizations to embark on both of these initiatives at the same time and even to use a combined Center of Excellence.

Time-to-Market

SOA delivers on reduced time-to-market in several ways. Composing solutions from existing assets, reusing services and processes, configuring processes and services to alter their behavior, and leveraging services and processes developed by third parties enable rapid solution development. While the vision of perfect reuse is not often realized, modifying or configuring an existing process or service is still cheaper, faster, and less risky than a new development effort.

Visibility

For many enterprises, the technology organization is a black hole into which money is shoveled in hopes that e-mail will be available and the corporate web site will remain available. There is little to no visibility into the actual technology capabilities that are available. Increasingly, this leads to business leaders making strategic decisions that are incongruent with existing infrastructure, capacity, and near-term capabilities. If the enterprise is looking at 30 potential opportunities in the marketplace and they will select four of them to pursue in the next calendar year, they have no insight into which opportunities are more or less feasible from an information systems perspective. Through a combination of service orientation, enterprise portfolio management, enterprise architecture, and business process alignment, visibility can be provided into the existing and near-term technology capabilities. This could likely drive the leadership to select four different opportunities for the calendar year. Visibility crystallizes existing and potential value and leads to increased awareness of technology ROI. On the other hand, this visibility can also lead to increased scrutiny regarding technology investments and the value or lack of value derived from them.

Modernization

SOA is a disruptive force that is changing the enterprise landscape in terms of technology, organizational strategies, and strategic business alignment. The disruptive nature of SOA is not unlike the disruption the world experienced from the Internet in the late 1990s. Interest in web sites, e-mail, and eventually e-commerce skyrocketed. Having a web address was a crucial litmus test for whether a company was "for real" or, according to some, whether a company was "with it." With few exceptions, these early sites did essentially nothing. They were glorified marketing brochures (i.e., "About Us," "Products," "Services," "Contact Us," etc.) displayed electronically within browsers. The value of having a site was rather marginal initially, but it grew increasingly important as additional innovations (i.e., e-commerce, portals, communities, collaboration, B2B integration, etc.) were ushered in and made available via the Web.

Similar to the disruptive impact of the Internet, SOA is changing the modern business landscape. As a result of SOA and related initiatives, there is less and less appetite for proprietary connectors in order to connect systems. There is less tolerance for long solution development cycles, brittle architecture, and inflexible systems. All major vendors and most minor vendors now ship their products with SOA-ready interfaces. Increasingly, business partners and vendors assume that XML and related SOA messaging standards represent a baseline for system-to-system communication. Reuse, agility, and interoperability are the order of the day, and many enterprises are beginning to recognize that adoption of SOA is necessary in order to stay current with the pace of business.

SURGICAL ADOPTION OF SOA

One important caveat to point out and something that will be explored at length later (see Chapter 5, "Is SOA Right for You?," and Chapter 9, "How Much SOA Do I Need?") is that adopting SOA is not an all-or-nothing proposition. While it is important to consider SOA adoption in order to remain current and not get left behind, this does not mean that every aspect of the enterprise should be service oriented. SOA is a disruptive technology, but blanket adoption across the board is a guaranteed way to ensure that SOA disrupts your enterprise business and may in fact result in jeopardizing certain mission-critical business processes. SOA should be adopted at a strategic level and then surgically applied at an operational and tactical level as appropriate.

CASE STUDY: SOA VALUE PROPOSITION

Taking a look at our Return Handling and Expense Approval case studies outlined earlier, we can better understand the SOA value proposition within a real-world context.

SOA Value for the *Return Handling* Case Study

Service orientation holds value for MO1, our mail-order company, by reducing the cost and hurdles associated with system integration and by introducing business agility and an opportunity to optimize and automate existing business processes. For example, if a product has been returned because it was damaged during shipping, an electronic business process orchestration will automatically ask the shipping carrier service to file a claim. The orchestration knows the context (the original order placed by the customer) and is able to automatically fetch all the information required by the shipping carrier, such as the waybill number and the account number, through a well-defined service interface. Additionally, in the event that this process must change or new systems must be brought online, these changes can be quickly and easily absorbed into the current service-oriented enterprise via updates to services, processes, or both.

SOA Value *Expense Approval* Case Study

HighTree, our IT training company, is currently dependent on multiple human activities to handle expense claims. In addition to the inherent bottlenecks that are present, there is no tracking mechanism and no means of escalating expense claims to another person in order to move the process along. SOA offers HighTree increased visibility into its business operations, the ability to substitute one actor for another (by escalating an expense claim to a manager for approval), and a means of integrating various disparate systems into a cohesive solution. The end result is a smoother business process and more rapid and accurate approval of expense claims. Additionally, the solution provides complete tracking and audit capabilities to ensure that nothing slips through the cracks.

SUMMARY

Identifying a value proposition for adoption of SOA is a multidimensional activity. Reducing integration expenses is key for any enterprise with significant technology assets. Reusing capabilities rather than recreating them each time is becoming increasingly important. Ensuring that the business is agile and able to adapt to changing demands is a virtual requirement in order to remain competitive. Risk reduction is on the radar for every business leader. SOA delivers in all four of these areas. Finally, the value for SOA adoption may simply be that disruptive technologies come along every seven to ten years and enterprises must adapt or watch their market share erode.

NOTE

1. To read the full ZapThink report, "The ROI of SOA," check out: www.zapthink.com/report.html?id=ZAPFLASH-20050127.

CHAPTER 4

RISKS IN SOA ADOPTION

At the time of this writing (2007), service oriented architecture (SOA) is not a proven, battle-tested concept. We must have a frank and open discussion about what can go wrong with it.

In the analysis presented here, many of the risks come from the inherent problems with information technology (IT) today. This chapter will lay the groundwork by explaining these problems. Then the unique problems that SOA might engender will be examined.

WHY DO WE USE TECHNOLOGY?

Since the very beginning of commerce, businesses have used tools and technologies to increase production levels. The simple mantra is that one human being can produce a lot more with the aid of tools. The tools do the repetitive tasks at a faster rate and more accurately than a human can. Humans control these tools and perform some of tasks that the tools cannot perform.

The Industrial Revolution saw the mass-scale application of this principle. Prior to this age, machines were powered by human beings (and in rare cases wind or water). This simple fact limited the per-capita production level. In the industrial age, machines are powered by steam, gasoline, or electricity. This has allowed a small number of people to run a vast array of machines.

For any kind of technology to be economically successful, two conditions have to be met:

1. The initial investment of procuring and installing the machines plus the day-to-day running cost must be offset by the increased revenue from the higher production levels.
2. Within a country or geographical region, the higher profit margins of the companies must create more jobs than the number of jobs cut due to automation. In other words, technology must automate as well as increase living standards of people. Without that, automation will run into opposition from the trade unions, or society in general.

Effectively, the second condition depends on the first. If technology increases profit, businesses have more capital to reinvest. Successful reinvestment causes growth and creates jobs. Reduced cost of production also lowers price of goods and improves living standards.

IT AS A TOOL

The computer was initially used by business as a means of record keeping. Once it replaced the ledger books, a small number of people could store and look up vast numbers of records. A company now knew exactly the inventory on hand and the status of orders.

The computer was next used to analyze the records that it was keeping. This yielded important insights into a company's business. A business could optimize its supply chain and achieve a just-in-time operation.

However, a dark cloud soon began to appear. Businesses used different software systems to keep records of different areas of the business. The accounting software that kept track of orders, invoices, and payments was distinct from the manufacturing management system that kept track of parts inventory and status of work items. And yet, one business process can rarely function with the services of a single software system. For example, we need a software that takes the order from the customer. We need the accounting system to send invoices and receive partial payment. Only then can we begin manufacturing. Once manufacturing ends, we need to obtain full payment before we can ship the item.

A business is now faced with two separate problems:

1. Who will enter all the records in each system? Many of the records are kept in more than one system. Manually entering data into one system by reading it off another one is slow and fraught with error. A single software product may be a great time-saving tool in its own area of concern, but we cannot say the same for a collective of software. In other words, the whole is less than the sum of its parts.

2. Who will coordinate the activities of a business process? For example, who checks for orders for which partial payments have been received and creates work orders in the manufacturing system? Certainly, trained employees can do this. Managers can oversee the overall compliance to the business process and mitigate any problems arising from human errors. Manual control of the process flow is feasible for a small number of process instances. As a business grows there will be more occurrences of trigger events that start a process. The volume of process instances will grow. Very soon overseeing so many activities will become humanly impossible or very slow.

IT's success in solving these problems has not been confirmed.[1] More software was developed to integrate systems and implement business processes. A multitude of software, each product using a different data format and communication protocol, is patched together. The integration logic is often complex, poorly documented, and too risky to change.

In summary, software excels at a small scale, automating individual tasks. But, when multiple tasks need to be threaded together in a business process, the current software design methodology and technology fall short.

The Crisis in IT

In her paper titled "The Trouble with Enterprise Software,"[2] Cynthia Rettig portrays a damning picture of the current state of IT. She specifically cites complexity of today's enterprise software as the primary source of the problems. Software by nature is not a true thinking machine. Instead, all possible conditions must be explicitly coded. By some measure, a 25% increase in complexity of a task causes 100% increase in complexity of the software. Every possible variation in the software's behavior represents the decision-making process of a human employee or the organization. It is coded using an if-then-else construct. When you look at the permutation of all if-then-else constructs in a software, you get an incredibly large number of possible variations.

We need to understand these inherent problems with IT, for they have the biggest influence on sabotaging SOA's success. For the purpose of our discussion, we will focus on a set of key problems.

- **Changing software is risky and slow.** Business operations are increasingly being automated through software. When the business decides to do things differently, the change needs to be reflected in the appropriate software. Mobilizing IT and taking the changes through testing and deployment is a slow process. It is difficult to judge the impact a change will have in the rest of the software and other software systems. Changes can introduce defects that are completely unanticipated.

- **Quality of the software.** Every software contains defects. In some cases, organizations do not follow proper testing process. Even if they did, testing for all possible scenarios is extremely difficult. In general, software lacks engineering-based practices similar to what you see in other disciplines such as mechanical, civil, and electrical engineering. In these disciplines, people carefully follow well-established practices, many of which are codified by regulations. In contrast, the software industry follows fad-based practices. Frameworks, tools, programming languages, and methodologies are invented on a steady basis. These assets often lack proper research backing their usefulness. That does not stop IT from using these assets. That is like a building contractor using a structural design technique after reading about it in a magazine.

- **Quality of the data.** The same records are often kept in multiple software systems. Each system uses a different format and convention. For example, one system uses abbreviated country codes (like US and CA) and the other uses a numbering scheme (15 for US, etc.). Also, every software identifies the same entity using a different primary key identifier. For example, the client "Bob's Hardware Inc." may have an ID of 1001 in accounting and 2005 in the warehouse. In addition, people enter invalid data that when copied into other systems causes major breakdowns.

- **Software and operational variability.** A software product can deal with a fixed set of conditions. This, initially, jives well with a manager's dream that an operation will follow a fixed well-defined process. Any variability, as every manager knows, is an enemy of quality and efficiency. The reality, however, is quite different. It is true that in manufacturing you can eliminate variability to a great extent. In other industries, variability is a fact of life. Variability is most rampant in industries where human customers play a direct role in the process (such as car rentals and restaurants). Software, inherently, has problems dealing with variability.

With this backdrop in mind, we will now see how well SOA fares at solving these problems.

BARRIERS TO SOA'S PROMISES

In the most optimistic estimation, SOA will solve most of the pressing information management problems. In the worst case, SOA is a temporary fad. This fear is not entirely unfounded. New software frameworks and methodologies pop up almost on a monthly basis. Cynics may even hint at a concerted effort by the vendors to sell old wine in a new bottle. The reality probably involves all of the above. It is our job, as savvy customers, to look behind the marketing hype and separate the wheat from the chaff. We will now attempt to do precisely that. We will take a critical look at various claims of SOA and analyze how justified they are.

SOA Will Bring Business and IT Together

The COBOL programming language made a similar claim. Later, when the object-oriented (OO) development paradigm was introduced, the requirements-gathering and analysis phase was meant to connect the business with IT. Neither of these have worked very well. What does SOA bring to the table that is new? The answer is *business process management (BPM)*. BPM works as the foundation and starting point of an SOA-based software development project. This is the first time IT has borrowed a purely management concept and added it to its task pipeline. In SOA, BPM is a closed-loop (feedback-driven) process. When a process orchestration is deployed into operation, it begins to gather *key performance indicators (KPIs)*. The managers monitor the KPIs and then suggest further changes to the process. This should make the managers firmly aware of what IT is doing, more than ever before.

Having said that, we cannot help but observe that SOA is mostly a technology vendor push. There is hardly any discussion on SOA in management publications like *MIT Sloan Management Review* and *Harvard Business Review*. And many of the articles that do appear are not flattering to SOA. Compare this with the way IT vendors are spewing out a plethora of articles and seminars on SOA. They are the ones who have invested billions of dollars in SOA products. They are the ones with a vested interest.

> SOA is largely about vendor push as they rush up a food chain that is being commoditized underneath them. It provides a nice way to pull business from EAI (Enterprise Application Integration) vendors and integrators into the arms of the platform vendors. —Brenda Michelson, Program Director, SOA Consortium, OOPSLA'07, October 21–25, 2007, Montréal, Québec, Canada

At the time of this writing, SOA simply has not been studied well from a management perspective. Without a foundation of management theory, SOA will be yet another technology play that claimed but failed to bring management and IT together. You must fill this gap in management studies if your organization is considering SOA. Either through internal research or by using independent management consultants (outside the influence of IT), you must answer these and more questions:

- What role will the business managers play, before and after an SOA-based infrastructure is deployed into operation?
- Can you validate, using proven management principles and practices, the changes SOA claims to bring to your organization? Are these changes required and strategic for the organization?

SOA Will Automate Business Processes

Automated business process, or *orchestration*, is perhaps the very reason for the existence of SOA. Since the beginning of time, the focus has been to automate individual tasks. Now we are moving into a new world where the entire business process (which is a sequence of tasks) is automated. In this world, the entire business becomes akin to a machine. Its internal operations, its interaction with the customers, partners, and suppliers, execute in a clockwork fashion in a never-ending symphony. Companies that make this transition early will enjoy a solid advantage over the companies that manually control processes. Yet, there are significant barriers to automating a process. Do not believe for a second that it will be easy. It will take a near-heroic effort from the business leaders and IT to enter this world.

To begin with, not all business processes are well defined. The Capability Maturity Model states five levels of process orientation for a company (see Chapter 2, "Business Process Management and SOA" for details). A business process has to be at least at level 3—*well defined*—before it can be automated. Companies that are serious about process automation should wait for a process to achieve level 4. At this level, the company has a formal methodology and assigned roles and responsibilities for defining and managing business processes. Before you think that you can automate processes, find out how process oriented your company is. If you are not ready for process automation, you may not be ready for SOA.

In some situations, business processes may be already automated using software code built inside the existing applications. This code may be spread over several applications. Are you willing to rip and replace these business processes and rebuild them the SOA way?

Human tasks present a serious problem. Not all tasks can be automated through software. SOA vendors have a way to include human tasks in an automated business process. At the time of this writing, every vendor does this in its own proprietary way and no standard exists. Most vendors provide a task inbox and outbox to implement human tasks. For example, in the Return Handling case study, an employee looks at a list of returned packages that need to be touched up and repackaged. The employee claims a task and begins to work on it. Alternatively, she can scan the barcode on the package, which automatically informs the system that the package is being worked on. When the work is done, the employee marks the task as completed. Expect to develop a lot of such front-end user interfaces to support human tasks. These applications need to be deployed wherever you have human staff working.

Services Will Be Reusable

In SOA, a business software is wrapped in a service. The service is capable of performing a set of tasks. A consumer of the service asks the service to perform these tasks. In most cases, automated business processes or orchestrations will be the consumers. SOA promises that once a service is developed, new business processes can use them as-is. This reusability of services allows IT to respond quickly to a change in business process or automate a new business process.

For a service to be reusable, a few conditions have to be met.

- **Completeness of capability.** A service must be capable of performing a task that a business process needs done. For example, in the Return Handling case study, the business process needs to refund the customer for the returned goods. If the accounting system service is capable of performing that task, the business process can simply ask the service to do it. Otherwise, the service needs to be enhanced to support that task.
- **Universality.** Each consumer of a service may expect the service to perform a task in a slightly different way. For example, the accounting system service may already support a task to refund a customer. However, the way the refund is done may not be acceptable to a business process. This makes the accounting system service nonreusable. A service is reusable only if it is more or less universal.
- **Interoperability.** A few technical conditions must exist before the consumer can use a service. For example, if the service supports an encrypted protocol, the consumer must be able to support the same protocol.

Out of these conditions, completeness of capability is self-explanatory and requires little elaboration. We must spend a little bit of time on the other two conditions. In her paper, Cynthia Rettig makes a case that the complexity of software makes it hard for a service to be universal. Reusability is possible on a small scale. Software developers have used libraries of pre-built code to cut down development time. But services hide large amounts of code. Each task supported by a service involves a lot of business logic and many possible variations. Not all the possible outcomes will be acceptable to all consumers of the service. Not all services can achieve a one-size-fits-all goal.

The software industry has been trying to achieve interoperability for a long time. The discipline that generally covers this effort is known as *distributed computing*. In this programming model, you could develop a server software module using a certain programming language and one vendor's technology and the client using another programming language running on another vendor's platform. Technologies such as RPC (Remote Procedure Call), CORBA (Common Object Request Broker Architecture), and EJB (Enterprise JavaBean) are examples of distributed computing. On paper, they had the right goals in mind. In the end, infighting among the vendors and excessive complexity of some of these technologies prevented the delivery of the interoperability that IT needed in real life. Against this backdrop of decades of failure, one cannot help but marvel at the unprecedented level of interoperability that Web Services has achieved. Web Services are built using open standards like XML and SOAP. The stunning simplicity of these technologies has fueled the adoption of Web Services. One can develop a Web Services provider (server) and consumer (client) with very little effort and without any expensive vendor software platform.

However, once you go down the Web Services path, you will soon find yourself in uncharted territory. Certainly, a simple Web Service is inherently interoperable. More advanced Web Services, on the other hand, that must support security, reliable delivery, and transaction will find it hard to be interoperable. The standards in these areas are still evolving. Not all SOA vendors support all standards or support them completely.

The interoperability problem is a temporary one. Vendors are sincerely working hard to produce the standards necessary for enterprise-grade services and support these standards with their products. Universality of services is then the only major roadblock for a service to be reusable.

Services Can Be Composed Like LEGO® Blocks

With LEGO® blocks, most pieces can be coupled with any other piece. This is possible because the pieces use a uniform coupling interface. In SOA, this metaphor is important. For example, let us say that you have business processes that use the accounting system for invoicing and payment. If you design the accounting system service properly, we should be able to replace the current accounting software with a new one and not have to change the business processes. After all, as long as the new accounting software is capable of processing invoices and payments, the vendor of the software is of little concern to the business process. This is a totally valid argument and SOA, quite rightfully, tries to achieve this goal. Exhibit 4.1 shows how a service can be replaced with an equivalent one without changing a business process that uses the service.

For a service to be replaceable, it must follow a service design principle known as *abstraction*. According to this principle, you must design the interface of the service to be completely independent of the underlying software vendor. That means that the names of the operations (tasks performed by the service) and the input/output data required by these operations must be completely vendor generic. These generic attributes will then need to be mapped to attributes that are specific to the underlying software. A business process interacts with the service using the generic interface. This generic interface is designed by keeping your business in mind. When you replace the underlying software of a service with a new vendor's software, we can keep the interface the

EXHIBIT **4.1** *As long as two services support the same interface or set of tasks, they are completely interchangeable to a business process that uses the service*

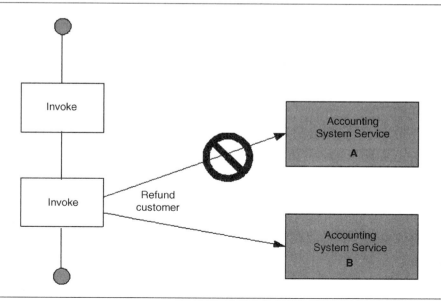

same. Thereby, the generic interface shields the business process from the newly adopted software.

There are numerous benefits to this rip-and-replace paradigm of service. Consider the cases where you may have to replace a software system or add a new one:

- You outsource certain operations to another company.
- Your company merges with or acquires another one and you need to integrate its accounting and human resources (HR) systems within your existing processes.
- Your warehouse operations have grown in complexity and new software is needed to address the problems.
- You have found a better supplier and want to use it as soon as possible.

While it is not hard to appreciate the potential gains of service abstraction, the reality may be quite different. LEGO® blocks are rather simple devices of similar shapes and sizes. It is not difficult to have them all conform to the same coupling interface. Also, there is no real interaction between the pieces (there is no flow of electricity, fluid, or data). A software system is vastly more complex. An accounting system from Oracle is utterly different from a similar system from J.D. Edwards. Replacing one with the other is equivalent to replacing the engine of a car with a new one. Arguably, a car expects the same set of services from its engine and one should be able to build a generic interface for the engine. In reality, the number and types of connections between an engine and the car can vary widely. Such is also the case for software systems.

Furthermore, you can safely anticipate that when you incorporate a new software system, there will also be a few changes to your company's core business processes. Outsourcing operations, mergers, and acquisitions are major events in the life of a business. Their impact can change certain practices of the business in fundamental ways. By definition, business process orchestrations are true digital reflections of the company's operations. SOA can do nothing to shield the existing orchestrations from such changes.

In conclusion, service abstraction is a valuable and important feature of SOA. It will certainly help ease the pain when you are changing software applications or integrating a new one. However, the complexity of the software and impact of life-altering events of a business should not be trivialized. In the end, SOA may only nominally lower IT's effort in dealing with these changes.

Open Standards Will Speed Up Application Integration

Standardization makes a service interoperable. We have already discussed interoperability as a condition for service reuse. Consider a scenario where you wish to do business with a new supplier. If that supplier offers a Web Service to query pricing and place orders, your IT will be able to readily start using that service and integrate the supplier to your business.

Web Services use standards like XML and SOAP. Unfortunately, not all services are Web Services. Most legacy enterprise applications do not expose their functionalities using Web Services. Vendors of these software packages are only beginning to support Web Services. Traditionally, interaction with these applications has been done using a component known as an *adapter*.

Most SOA vendors provide tools to quickly generate adapter-based services from these adapters. Exhibit 4.2 shows how an adapter-based service works.

EXHIBIT **4.2** *An adapter-based service is created using the adapter for the software*

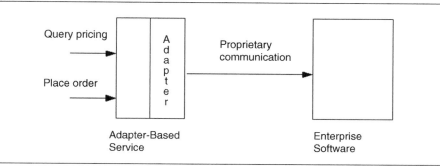

An adapter-based service is more standard compliant than a plain adapter. For example, the service uses XML and WSDL. But, it does not use SOAP. Depending on the vendor, an adapter-based service supports just enough standard for it to be usable by a business process orchestration. An orchestration treats all services in a uniform manner. A service may be a Web Service, a human task, an adapter-based service, or another orchestration.

An adapter-based service is interoperable with a consumer that is developed using the same SOA platform as the service itself. For example, if you build the adapter-based service using Oracle, the orchestration must also be developed using Oracle. This may be an acceptable limitation in the beginning. After all, chances are high that you will adopt a single SOA vendor. Eventually, you will face two problems:

1. In a large organization, you may have divisions that use a different SOA vendor. They will not be able to use your adapter-based services.
2. You may have a business partner that wishes to use your service. Once again, that will be possible only if the other organization uses the same SOA platform as yours.

You must make your services fully interoperable to solve these problems. Of course, that means you need to create Web Services. There are three options when it comes to exposing a legacy application as a Web Service:

1. You can develop your own Web Service. This service acts as liaison between the consumer and the legacy enterprise software.
2. An SOA platform vendor can automatically expose an adapter-based service as a Web Service.
3. You can wait for your legacy software's vendor to natively support Web Services.

Exhibit 4.3 shows options 1 and 2.

To summarize, just because someone tells you that SOA uses standards that make services easy to integrate into your IT infrastructure

EXHIBIT **4.3**   *An adapter-based service can be front-ended by a Web Service to make the service more standard compliant*

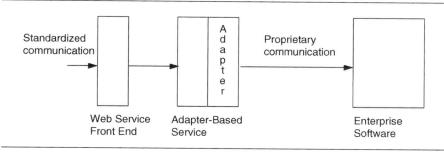

does not mean that is true. Not all services are standards based. Creating adapter-based services is easy. Many organizations will be tempted to do so. Unfortunately, they cannot be used from a different vendor's SOA platform. It is possible to convert the adapter-based services to Web Services and we have pointed out three approaches to do so. But, that will require extra work and expenses.

Business Will Be Able to React Faster to Variability

It has been much touted that SOA makes a business more agile. Traditionally, IT has been the bottleneck between the business brains to come up with an idea and the business to actually implement that idea. Can SOA really reduce that time lag?

There are two types of changes within an organization where SOA can play a role:

1. Changes to the business processes, for example, changes in the order in which tasks are performed.
2. Changes to the players in the business processes. Examples of this type of change include replacing a supplier organization with a new one, outsourcing the call center, and acquisition of a small company.

In the second type of change, a new player (or a service) is integrated into the business processes. SOA eases this effort by means of service abstraction and standardization. That is, if the business processes deal with the services in an abstract manner and the services follow standardized communication protocol, we can reduce the time it takes to integrate a new player into the organization. We have already discussed service abstraction and standardization in great length elsewhere. Here, we will focus on the first type of change—changes to a business process.

BPM requires that you continuously optimize a business process. Changes are made in order to achieve lower cost of operation, higher quality of output, fewer mistakes, and better customer satisfaction. According to SOA, if the business process changes, you should be able to simply alter the orchestration and put it in practice. You should not have to alter the underlying services or software applications. Changes to a business process can be put into practice without altering any service only if the following two conditions exist:

1. The altered business process does not need to perform any task that no service can currently perform.
2. The altered process does not need changes to be made to the way a task is currently performed.

In other words, as long as the new business process keeps to using the existing library of services, it will be relatively painless to deploy it. In the early phases of SOA adoption, when the collection of services within your organization is small and immature, condition 1 will be routinely violated. You will find yourself continuously adding functionality to existing services or creating new ones. Arguably, this problem is a temporary one. Over a period of time, the services will mature.

Condition 2, however, is a real problem. An orchestration employs relatively simple business logic to control the sequence of tasks. The bulk of the business logic resides in software applications. For example, if you wish to change the pricing logic, you will need to do that in your product catalogue software and not in a business process. Changes to software application take time and are highly risky. We have already identified that as one of the main problems that IT is facing. SOA can do nothing to help you there.

OTHER RISKS

So far we have discussed factors that can sabotage SOA from delivering on its promises. On top of that, SOA itself, due to its very nature, brings in new risks. That is not to say that SOA is an unsound idea. Any technology or thought process has weaknesses. We must know what they are, be vigilant about them, and find ways to deal with them.

Immature Standards

Standardization makes a service readily usable by a consumer. Let us say that you are a manufacturer. A new dealer will be able to quickly integrate you into its order processing system if your organization provides a standards-based service. Without standardization, the dealer will have to write a lot of custom code just for you.

SOA, not surprisingly, puts a lot of emphasis on standardization. Some of the earlier standards, such as, XML, SOAP, and HTTP have been successful. But, these standards are only the tip of the iceberg. We need standards around a whole slew of other areas, such as security, encryption, compression, transaction, and guaranteed delivery of messages (see the Appendix, "Standards in SOA," for more details). The need for these technologies is well understood by the software developers. They are not new by any means. The need for standardization is new. Going back to our example, if the dealer sends an encrypted message, the manufacturer's service should know how to decrypt it. What if not all dealers use message encryption? In that case, the manufacturer needs to set up different policies. The dealer needs to specify the policy that applies to it. This exchange of policy information, like all communication between two parties, also needs to be standardized.

While SOA emphasizes standardization, many of the standards are either missing or in an early stage. Immature standards are often not followed by the SOA platform vendors or are otherwise not interoperable between vendors. And, noninteroperable standards are as good as no standard at all.

When a standard for a technology is lacking, SOA practitioners are tempted to not use that technology. That is an extremely dangerous trap. Technologies like encryption, transaction, and guaranteed delivery are pillars that strengthen the IT infrastructure. The last thing you should do is to compromise the quality of your IT systems because your SOA vendor does not support certain standards.

Immature SOA Platforms

SOA is not a revolutionary new concept. It is an evolution of enterprise application integration and distributed computing. The productization of SOA, however, is new. Major vendors such as IBM, BEA, and TIBCO have only recently started offering SOA products. In many cases, these large vendors started their SOA product line by purchasing smaller companies. Products from these smaller companies simply did not have the robustness and scalability demanded by the enterprises.

In recent years, we have personally worked with several SOA platforms. We found the fragility of these systems simply alarming. To be fair, the vendors are working hard to make the products better. New versions of the SOA products are generally released at a faster rate than the traditional middleware systems like databases.

When choosing an SOA platform, look out for these areas of weakness:

- **Stability.** Immature products can crash under stress.
- **Performance.** Web Services were never meant to exchange large amounts of data. Consequently, SOA shines when you exchange small amounts of data in real time. Most SOA platforms I have worked with will not handle large data transfers efficiently. Transferring and converting volumes of data require specialized software development techniques. If you do intend to deal with large amounts of data, make sure your SOA platform can handle it.
- **Scalability and availability.** Clustering allows running your SOA platform on multiple machines. Besides being able to handle more

load, multiple hardware also gives you high availability. Make sure that your SOA platform meets your clustering needs.

- **SOA methodology compliance.** Does your SOA vendor's platform support concepts like service abstraction? How about top-down service development? The top-down approach, where a service is made to strictly conform to a specification, is considered to be a best practice by many. For some major vendors, we found out to our dismay that top-down development is not possible.

  Some vendors are adding SOA capability to their EAI products almost as an afterthought. In that case, the simple task of using a Web Service from an orchestration can be complicated.

- **Quality of support.** Mature software provides excellent problem-determination tools. Today, these tools are sorely lacking in many vendors' SOA platform.

We advise you to first use an SOA platform in a noncritical business process. Slowly start moving to more core business processes as you gain more confidence in the tools.

Added Complexity in Testing

This is not a problem with SOA per se. Any framework that builds a solution using many software applications, business partners, and customers is extremely hard to test. If you already have been doing EAI, you will know that.

> Technically, I have seen in my projects (having the size of up to 10 million service calls a day) two major technical problems: First, there is a tradeoff between performance and reusability. Second, testing becomes incredibly difficult because due to the distribution of the processes you have to prepare for distributed testing which implies that all stake holders have to prepare corresponding test data and that the infrastructure (the enterprise service bus) becomes your debugger. —Nicolai M. Josuttis, independent system architect, technical manager, author, and consultant, OOPSLA'07, October 21–25, 2007, Montréal, Québec, Canada

SOA Does Little to Improve Software Quality

SOA is not a methodology that will lower the number defects in software. If anything, it will make things worse. This argument stems from the fact that SOA is the glue that ties together existing software. Your SOA solution will be as good or as buggy as these underlying systems.

If you already have an unstable and unreliable IT framework, the new code developed to implement SOA will merely add to the misery.

SUMMARY

In most industries, such as civil engineering, aerospace, and healthcare, uniformity of practice happens at three different levels:

1. At the very core foundation, we have scientific theories. They firmly establish the principles that guide the industry practices. These theories are proposed using the age-old scientific method of observation of phenomena, formulation of hypotheses, validation these hypotheses using tests, and finally approval of the theories through peer review. If you are a civil engineer in charge of designing a bridge, you will compute the stress level on the component using well-established principles. You will not do anything based on a few articles you have read in the trade journals.

2. In some industries, scientific principles are codified for ease of use. For example, in shipbuilding, complex engineering calculations are reduced to simpler algebraic formulas. Using these codes, you can calculate values like the thickness of steel plate, the size and shape of the brackets, and the number of bulkheads. Codification can be done by the government, insurance companies, or an industry body.

3. Finally, standardization takes place. Standardization is usually driven by the vendors and controlled by an industry body. For example, the American Society for Testing and Materials (ASTM) standardizes the composition of elements in steel. If your

design calls for "ASTM A414 Grade F" steel, you can procure that from any number of steel manufacturers.

The software trade is in a serious crisis today, because it has not developed like the other industries. Software engineering schools are weak. They have failed to produce any scientific theories and principles for software development. If they have, no one in the industry knows about them. Certainly, no one follows them.

SOA emphasizes standardization. But, that will merely put a beautiful veneer over ugly, complex, and defect-riddled legacy code. Do not turn to SOA to cure all of your IT ills. It will do best what it is designed to do—make application integration easier and automate business processes.

NOTES

1. By IT, I specifically mean software. We can leave hardware out of the discussions here. The reliability and capacity of hardware are more than adequate. We have seen little evidence of hardware as a contributing factor to IT's problems.
2. Cynthia Rettig, "The Trouble with Enterprise Software," *MIT Sloan Management Review*, Fall 2007, Vol. 49, No. 1.

IS SOA RIGHT FOR MY BUSINESS?

With a better understanding of service oriented architecture (SOA) and the positive and negative consequences associated with it, you naturally want to know whether it is applicable to your business. SOA is not one-size-fits-all. There are some industries, business processes, and circumstances that truly warrant SOA. There are others that simply are not a good fit. The chapters in this part of the book shed light on this vital subject.

Chapter 5, "Is SOA Right for You?," introduces scenarios where SOA is commonly a good fit (i.e., application integration, process automation, distributed computing, etc.). SOA feasibility is explored in this chapter from several angles, including skills availability, performance requirements, and technology capabilities.

Chapter 6, "Applying SOA to Various Industries," examines real-world SOA through the lens of 25 enterprises that have adopted SOA, spread across five industry sectors (defense, finance, media, technology, and travel). Guidance is provided regarding the application of SOA to other sectors and specific industries not mentioned.

Chapter 7, "Calculating SOA ROI," highlights the challenges associated with identifying and measuring a return on investment (ROI) for SOA. This chapter defines three types of ROI (tactical, operational, strategic) and provides practical guidance regarding calculating the value for each category. Specific calculation models are provided where applicable and the case studies are used to provide tangible examples.

CHAPTER 5

IS SOA RIGHT FOR YOU?

Service oriented architecture (SOA) solves a specific set of problems.
It simultaneously automates business processes and integrates applications. It is not a general-purpose software design technique. Even in
certain situations where two applications need to communicate, SOA
may not be the best option. This chapter will provide a few guidelines
around when not to adopt SOA.

MEASURING THE APPROPRIATENESS OF SOA

Do You Need Application Integration?

Does your business use separate software applications for accounting, human resources, payroll, and other purposes? Do you have
business processes that need to use more than one such software?
For large-to-medium businesses, the answer to these questions is invariably *yes*. SOA is an excellent choice to integrate applications. In
a few years, it may be the dominant approach as more and more *enterprise application integration (EAI)* vendors conform to SOA in
their products.

If, however, your business or division uses a small number of applications or the level of interaction between the applications is minimal,
SOA may not be a necessity.

Do You Want to Automate Interaction with Your Partners?

Automated interaction with your partners (customers, dealers, suppliers, and distributors) has many benefits. SOA emphasizes standardization. You and your partners can now adopt standards such as XML, SOAP, and Web Services to implement the interaction. This will make life easier for all parties. SOA also helps you abstract out partners. This will, for example, speed up the integration of a new customer or the replacement of a supplier.

If your business performs or intends to perform automated interaction with several external entities, SOA will be a compelling choice.

Do You Need Distributed Computing?

In SOA, applications interact with each other over the network. This type of programming leads to complex software setup. Tracking down a problem can be difficult. Performance of network communication is slower than the in-memory and in-process communication that objects use.

Do not replace object-oriented development with SOA. Objects and services have completely different purposes. Objects are made up of smaller amounts of code. In contrast, a service can be made up of an entire software or an organization. When the scope of the functionality is as large as a software or organization, service is a clear choice. The problem is with cases where a service is built to encompass only small amounts of business logic. Such small-scale services make sense only in certain scenarios:

- Does the functionality need to be used by software written using many different programming languages? If so, a service is a better option than an object.
- Does the functionality need to be exposed to your customers or suppliers? In this case, a service is a great idea. External organizations can access the functionality, over the Internet, without installing any special software that is specific to your business.

- Does the functionality change frequently? In that case, a service can centralize the code in one place. If you change the business logic of the service, its users can pick up the update automatically without going through a time-consuming upgrade process.

Do You Have the Skills?

Technologies, standards, and software used by SOA are not necessarily more complex than any other platform (such as J2EE or Microsoft's .NET). However, there is a perceived notion of complexity that largely stems from the fact that these components are fairly new. A considerable amount of retraining of your information technology (IT) staff will be needed before you can get started with SOA.

Can Your Applications Play Nice?

SOA will require you to create services for the existing software applications. There are several ways to create a service. The software may natively expose Web Services. The vendor may provide an adapter that you can use to build an adapter-based service.

Applications not only need to be able to accept messages, it may be necessary for them to send messages to other services. The latter is necessary when an application needs to notify others about key events (such as a customer record being updated).

In other words, SOA puts certain demands on an application before you can use that application in your SOA-based solution. It will be a smart move to verify whether most of your applications can satisfy these requirements. The "Technology Evaluation" section of this chapter will show you how to perform basic tests to validate whether a technology is appropriate for your organization.

Performance Is a Concern

Web Services excel at transferring small amounts of information. Within SOA platform software, a message is loaded into memory before it is transformed and processed. This makes SOA not so suitable for transferring very large messages. It will be a while before the SOA vendors explicitly design their products to handle bulk data transfer.

SOA is also not advisable for situations where high performance and near-real-time communication is important. SOA can be problem here for a few different reasons:

- XML messages are easy to process (for both humans and software). But, that comes with a performance penalty. XML messages tend to be larger than a message created in a proprietary format. High-performance software can and probably should use a custom non-XML format for speed.
- In SOA, the sender of a message never directly sends the message to the receiver. Messages flow through an SOA platform software that can add many extra layers. Layers such as data transformation, auditing, and business process state management can slow down performance.
- Finally, most SOA platform software today is fairly immature. Vendors are focusing on adding new features and supporting the standards. The products are generally not very well tuned out of the box. The body of knowledge regarding performance optimization is minimal, compared with mature technologies such as web servers and database servers.

If a solution calls for high performance and near-real-time data transfer, carry out a few proof-of-concept projects to make sure that these requirements can be satisfied using your SOA platform. Also consider employing an enterprise messaging system rather than XML Web Services.

Can the Business Processes Be Automated?

If your business processes are largely manual, document centric (exchanging messages via e-mail), or highly unstable (changing frequently), you may not see much benefit from SOA.

The interface of a service also has to be stable. How the service completes its tasks can change frequently. But, the structure of the incoming and outgoing messages should be fairly stable. Too many changes to the service interface adversely affect its consumers. Some level of flux is expected in the early days of a service. This should eventually stabilize. If, by nature, the interface of a service cannot be pinned down, SOA may not be the best option.

Do You Have a Business Case?

This is perhaps the most important criterion in deciding whether SOA is right for you. A business case or plan will document in detail the benefits you expect to see from SOA. A good business case will even include a return on investment (ROI) calculation. ROI prediction is notoriously difficult in IT. Do not let the complexity of ROI calculation bog you down and delay the creation of a business case.

At minimum, the business case will itemize the expected benefits or goals you intend to achieve using SOA. Each benefit must be validated using the following criteria:

- Is the benefit real? Is the goal you intend to achieve central to the business? Artificial goals and benefits may sound good on paper but will yield little value to the business.
- Are there any business roadblocks that can stop you from realizing the benefit?

For example, if you say that SOA will help you automate business process, apply simple tests such as these to validate that hypothesis:

- Are a majority of the tasks in a business process done manually? If so, automation of the process will not yield much benefit.
- Does the process vary wildly? If so, automation will not be possible.

Similarly, if you think SOA will make you agile, validate that assumption. If most changes in the business need changes to the code of the existing software applications, SOA will not make you any more agile than what you are today.

Chapter 4, "Risks in SOA Adoption," takes a critical look at each benefit of SOA and explains when you may or may not see that benefit. Use that chapter in conjunction with this one to formulate the validation tests in your business case.

Next, get the business case peer reviewed. People with different experience and viewpoints will validate the assumptions in different ways. Finally, you need to run small tests to prove your assumptions. We get into that next.

TECHNOLOGY EVALUATION

SOA is not an all-or-nothing proposition. SOA bundles many different technologies (see the Appendix, "Standards in SOA," for a list). It may not be possible to adopt every one of them in your business. Some of the benefits you have outlined in the business case may not be achievable for technical reasons. For example, if you think you can interact with your suppliers using Web Services, you need to make sure that:

- Most of your suppliers offer a Web Service today.
- You are able to consume these Web Services. This sounds unnecessary, but any number of issues can make it very difficult to use a Web Service. Unless you actually try it out, you will never know.

There are mainly two ways to test whether a business goal will be technically achievable through SOA. You can build a proof-of-concept solution. Such a solution should attempt to use the actual SOA platform of your organization and the services of your partners. That is perhaps the most conclusive way. However, procuring funding for throw-away software can be difficult. Alternatively, you can perform thorough research of your business partners' SOA infrastructure and the capabilities of your own SOA platform. This will yield a "best effort" estimate of whether a specific SOA technology will work well in the context of your business.

The finding from this exercise will feed back into the business case. For failure of a test can mean an unrealized business benefit of SOA. Exhibit 5.1 shows the feedback process.

EXHIBIT **5.1** *Small projects verify whether there are any technical road-blocks to your SOA plan*

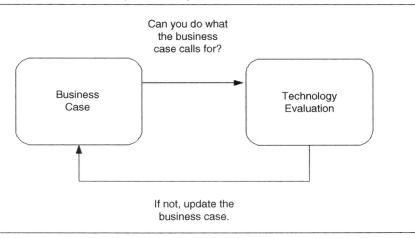

In the paper titled "Four Pillars of Service-Oriented Architecture,"[1] Lewis and Smith of Carnegie Mellon University provide a guideline for testing suitability of an SOA standard or technology. It proposes a five-step process:

Step 1. From the business case document, identify the need for a technology. Determine the environment for that technology. The environment will include items such as the SOA vendor's tool and programming language.

Step 2. Develop hypotheses that are based on the expectations derived from the business case. For example, if the business case says SOA should help us quickly replace one supplier with another, the hypothesis will say something like, "We should be able to integrate a new supplier without changing the code of any software applications."

Step 3. Develop concrete criteria for each hypothesis that will validate the outcome of the test. These criteria should be clearly measurable so that the tests are conclusive.

Step 4. Design and implement a proof-of-concept software solution that will help us validate the hypotheses. The solution is then run and observed until we can evaluate all the criteria.

Step 5. Run the test results through the criteria and find out if a hypothesis is valid.

At the end of the process, there should be enough evidence for you to come to one of these conclusions:

- A technology, standard, or vendor tool is suitable for your business.
- A technology, standard, or vendor tool is not suitable for your business.
- A technology, standard, or vendor tool has a few problems that can be worked around.

A few case studies will help:

Hypothesis	How to Prove
The new employee hire process can be automated.	Start by modeling the business process. Then apply these tests to verify that there are no business roadblocks to achieving the goal:
	• A peer review finds the business process accurate. If there are arguments about this, the process is most likely not very well understood and highly variable.
	• Most of the tasks in the business process can be automated through software. You need to clearly define what *most* means. It may be 80% or 70%.
	The business-level validation of a goal is done while developing the business case. Next comes the technology evaluation. Using your SOA vendor's tool, implement and execute a simplified version of the business process. This will prove that the technology works in the context of your business.

When an order is placed on the web site, the order should be automatically entered in the accounting system.

The technology evaluation of this goal can consist of the following tests:

- Build a Web Service or adapter-based service for the accounting system. This will validate that such a service can indeed be created.
- Build an order-processing business process. Call the accounting service from the process to enter an order.
- Start the business process from the web site when an order is placed.

Any one of these tests can fail for any number of reasons. Technology evaluation can save you from committing huge amounts of funding and staffpower on a project that is destined to fail for technical reasons.

When a customer's address changes in the sales system, it also should be changed in the accounting and the e-commerce system.

Create a proof-of-concept application as follows:

- Build a Web Service for the e-commerce and accounting system to update an address.
- Build a business process. It should be able to convert the address for the accounting and e-commerce systems.
- Have the sales system start the business process when an address is updated.

SUMMARY

Before you invest time and money into SOA, you must establish the validity of the architecture in the context of your organization. A business case is a good starting point. Every benefit you expect to see from SOA must be critically reviewed. Once the business case finds justification to go with SOA, you need to get down to more details and find out what specific technology and tool will work for your business. This two-step validation process will minimize any nasty surprises later in the life of an SOA project.

NOTE

1. Grace A. Lewis and Dr. Dennis B. Smith, "Four Pillars of Service-Oriented Architecture," *CrossTalk, Journal of Defense Software Engineering*, September 2007 issue. www.stsc.hill.af.mil/crosstalk/ 2007/09/0709LewisSmith.html.

CHAPTER 6

APPLYING SOA TO VARIOUS INDUSTRIES

Service orientation has been successfully applied to a wide range of enterprises in the private and public sectors. Organizations of all shapes and sizes have found service oriented architecture (SOA) to be a key ingredient in their information modernization and next-generation enterprises. Due to SOA's broad applicability to a variety of challenges in the modern enterprise, there are countless examples of SOA's applicability to various industries. This chapter will not attempt to address each one by any means. Instead, the aim is to address five major industry sectors and explore a couple of specific segments within each sector. Twenty-five specific examples of real-world SOA adoption will be highlighted. Finally, the chapter will conclude with some tips on how to apply SOA to other industries not mentioned in this material.

DEFENSE SECTOR

The U.S. Department of Defense (DOD) began an effort in the late 1990s to modernize information management and cross-entity collaboration.[1] This Network Centric Warfare (*network-centric* or simply *net-centric* for short) concept has evolved and matured over the years, encompassing more and more of the DOD's vision for next-generation warfare. The DOD's Global Information Grid (GIG), aimed at providing a common infrastructure for system and data integration, has also adopted this net-centric model.[2] The objective is to promote net-centric operations across service branches and intelligence agencies through a consistent architectural model and promote a culture of information sharing and capability reuse. In recent years, the net-centric initiative has evolved into a full-fledged and federated SOA for the entire DOD, with individual branches establishing independent but standards-based and interoperable SOA infrastructures.

Intelligence

The intelligence community has been going through a tremendous transformation since September 11, 2001. There is a keen realization that interoperability and collaboration are essential keys to succeeding in an information war. The problem is that this bucks against standard operating procedure for the intelligence community. The traditional model is to protect data at all costs, build tall walls (literally and meta-phorically) to create information silos, and dispense information only once a "need to know" has been established. While this effectively protects data, it is not conducive to the more collaborative and dynamic information exchange that is required for the modern global landscape.

Attitudes are changing now within the DOD community in a variety of ways:[3]

- "Information is power" is giving way to a mindset that understands and utilizes "the power of information."
- Breaking traditional information silos, organizations are starting to behave as stewards of information and not information owners.
- "Need to know" is out; "need to share" and "right to know" are in.

Consequently, SOA has taken center stage in enabling data sharing. The intelligence community is moving away from a reliance on client-specific software in favor of Web-based services. Agents are being empowered with access to data regardless of what agency or service branch originally owned the data. This is accomplished due to an emphasis on promoting data interoperability rather than application interoperability.

Initiatives like the Raytheon-led Distributed Common Ground System (DCGS) typify how SOA is being embraced by the defense intelligence community.[4] DCGS is charged with creating an information-sharing and capability-sharing backbone to connect together the various nodes of the intelligence community. XML-based metadata catalogs, well-defined data vocabularies, and standardized service-based interfaces facilitate real-time decision making with the best available data regardless of which agency or service branch serves as the steward of the data. Data enables effective decisions, but that data must be shared, discoverable, and relevant. SOA makes this a reality. Moving forward, SOA enables new capabilities to be fielded much more quickly, often through reuse, greatly increasing military agility.

Simulation

Inventor Edward Albert Link launched the simulation and training industry in 1929 when he filed for a patent on his legendary instrument flight trainer known as "the Blue Box." Since those early days, simulation has grown into a high-fidelity world of visual modeling, real-time battlefield simulation, and strategic and tactical mission training. In recent years, simulation devices have been networked together to enable collaborative battlefield simulation. One such example is L-3's Link Simulation and Training Division and their Aviation Combined Arms Tactical Trainer (AVCATT) program, which links up to four simulators into a single mission exercise.[5]

While programs like AVCATT are very capable, they are limited by physical proximity. All the simulation devices must be in one location and directly connected into the network. Although still in the Research and Development phase, next-generation simulation and training environments will be service oriented. This will manifest itself in two basic ways. First, the components themselves will be linked in modularly through standardized interfaces and XML-based protocols. Components such as the visual database, runtime system, mission brief/debrief,

Instructor Operator System (IOS), Learning Management System (LMS), and more can be assembled together as needed. If you want to link together multiple visual databases or replace one LMS with another, you can. The second way that next generation simulation and training environments will benefit from SOA is the ability to conduct distributed missions in real-time, introducing participants (both friend and foe) dynamically into the battlefield space.[6] Participants can exist anywhere in the world (office, training facility, deck of an aircraft carrier, etc.) and will be able to join and leave the battle space as needed. These actors can be full simulators, or even thin PC-based clients (think Unmanned Aerial Vehicles, specialized IOSs, individual enemy combatants, etc.).

FINANCIAL SECTOR

Probably the most celebrated examples of SOA transforming industry come from the financial sector. The process-centric nature of finance, and especially of the insurance industry, lends itself well to SOA. Agility and reuse, value propositions that financial organizations regard very highly, also point toward service orientation. Finally, enterprises in the financial sector tend to have a considerable collection of legacy systems due to the age of many of the organizations as well as the frequency of mergers and acquisitions within this sector.

Banking and Investments

Service orientation took root in banks and brokerages long before it was a mainstream, well-defined concept. Common themes include seamless access to data and business logic that was previously locked away in silos, reuse of systems and capabilities across business units, and service orientation of business processes to enable agility.

Consider the following cases of service orientation:

- **Improved business processes.** *Synovus,* a regional bank in the southeastern part of the United States with about $33 billion in assets, took a service oriented approach to its Internet banking and technology modernization initiatives.[7] It automated and streamlined nearly 30 manual processes using SOA and business process management (BPM) and did so under a very aggressive timeline. *Harley-Davidson Financial Services*, the financial services arm of Harley, focused their SOA initiative on building services around key business processes.[8] The emphasis was on loose coupling to provide the flexibility to change one part of a process without touching the other parts. To catch the spring marketing season, the processes of checking a potential buyer's credit and approving a loan to purchase a motorcycle are merged into a fluid, accelerated business process. Once summer arrives, the process is switched back to the more traditional, extended loan approval process.

- **Seamless data access.** *Merrill Lynch's Enterprise Data Solutions* unit has used SOA to enable an enterprise search-and-discovery portal capable of searching 34 million records across multiple systems.[9] Previously, users would have to juggle as many as 12 independent systems in order to manage accounts. Thanks to XML-based service interfaces and a service oriented abstraction layer, any client system can now seamlessly access the enterprise transaction systems through a common portal. *Farm Credit Services of America (FCSAmerica)*, based in Omaha, Nebraska, supplies roughly one-third of the U.S. agriculture industry's loans. FCSAmerica previously relied on nighttime batch processing to keep business information current across their mainframe-based loan accounting system, third-party customer relationship management (CRM) system, custom loan origination system written in Visual Basic, and their Web-based system dealer origination system written in Java. FCSAmerica was reaching capacity on nighttime batch processing, and transaction times for same-day loans were very slow due to personnel having to rekey information into multiple systems. Through SOA, the company deployed a shared-services CRM system to replace the tangle of point-to-point connections with a single, seamless view of enterprise data.[10]

- **Asset reuse.** *The Corporate and Investment Banking (CIB) division of Wachovia*, the fourth largest bank in the United States, observed that each business unit built similar capabilities (customer information management, data management, messaging, workflow logic, presentation logic, etc.) over and over.[11] CIB rolled out a comprehensive SOA infrastructure, reframed the relationship between business and IT to be more interactive and consultative, and restructured the organization to better facilitate service oriented championship. The end result is dramatically improved time-to-market and a competitive edge that has helped the bank win several significant contracts. Financial planning firm *Ameriprise Financial*, with more than $490 billion in assets, has saved millions of dollars through its SOA initiative.[12] It defines three service tiers: enterprise reuse, shared reuse, and specialized reuse. Its crown jewel is the customer management enterprise service, which has already delivered more than $10 million in savings.

Insurance

Another early adopter of SOA has been the insurance industry. Many of the same themes experienced on the banking and investment side of the financial sector appear here as well. Cost control through asset reuse, legacy system consolidation, and improved time to market through business and IT alignment are all key.

Some of the notable examples of SOA success from the insurance industry include:

- **Lower IT costs.** *Guardian Life Insurance*, the fourth largest mutual life insurance company in the United States, uses SOA to keep application development costs low and promote reuse.[13] The company set out to leverage its legacy assets and see how it could develop a service architecture on top of these systems to provide three key sets of capabilities: benefits administration, claims processing, and policyholder administration. Guardian's chief architect estimates that SOA has saved 30% of the application development budget. *Standard Life Group*,[14] in Edinburgh, Scotland, has seen significant savings result from its adoption of SOA. With more than 40% of the company's back-end transactions initiated through its SOA-based environment and extensive service reuse, the company has saved more than £2.8 million in development costs over a period of three years.

- **Seamless system integration.** *Blue Cross/Blue Shield of Massachusetts (BCBSMA)*, the largest health insurer in New England, has begun its SOA adoption efforts in order to move away from a vertical, silo-type approach to software and focus more on horizontal, enterprise capabilities.[15] The new infrastructure provides BCBSMA with a seamless, service-based fabric that abstracts the multiple back-office applications that comprise its legacy environment. SOA has also simplified the process of integrating partners into the company's enterprise systems and enabled it to provide customers with a seamless experience via a self-service Web portal. The company is now regarded as a leading player in the health-care industry.

- **Faster time to market.** *esure*, a prominent United Kingdom–based personal insurance carrier (one million policies and growing), turned to service orientation to drive faster time to market and closer alignment between business and IT.[16] Adopting SOA has yielded a 50% reduction in the number of hours needed to develop new solutions. New, flexible insurance ratings systems now allow underwriters to directly manage rates up to ten times faster than the previous system. Service orientation enables esure to react quickly to market changes and produce viable solutions sooner and more effectively.

MEDIA SECTOR

The media sector has two primary types of entities: traditional broadcasting and/or publishing outfits, and more modern digital media companies. SOA is beginning to take hold among traditional media companies and is already actively used by digital media companies.

Broadcasting and Publishing

Media powerhouse *British Broadcasting Corporation (BBC)* is incrementally service orienting its enterprise over a period of several years.[17] The objective is to develop an interoperable IT infrastructure that allows for legacy and future technologies to work well together. The BBC's SOA adoption strategy is targeting the following benefits:

- Reduce the total cost of ownership for IT.
- Create a more unified technology team.
- Reduce the number of applications and components.
- Improve information quality and availability to workers.

Over a period of nine years, the BBC plans to systematically replace point-to-point interfaces between silo-based systems in favor of modern, standards-based systems. The BBC's SOA will allow metadata to be exchanged across the organization and facilitate process change and better alignment between business and IT.

Digital and New Media

DreamWorks Animation, the studio behind *Shrek*, *Bee Movie*, and *Madagascar*, turned to SOA to simplify and consolidate key business operations.[18] DreamWorks began by replacing 12 legacy enterprise resource planning (ERP) systems with a layered and standards-compliant architecture. Through SOA component reuse, standard service protocols, and flexible business process models, it has realized a whole host of business improvements. The new environment is faster, sleeker, more manageable, and much more capable.

Sony Pictures Entertainment, which brought the world *Spider-Man*, *Hitch*, and *The Legend of Zero*, uses SOA to manage thousands of terabytes of digital assets.[19] Sony's digital asset management solution, cineSHARE, provides an interoperable, manageable, and scalable infrastructure of shared services to support digital asset management, media conversation, and a variety of content distribution processes. Sony has seen significant efficiency improvements, including reduced time-to-benefit (from months to weeks), as a result of service orientation.

TECHNOLOGY SECTOR

In case the technology sector did not have enough acronyms to contend with, nearly every technology industry has adopted SOA and the basket of acronyms that comes with it (XML, SOAP, WSDL, UDDI, BPEL, BPM, WS-Security, WS-Policy, etc.). Two technology industries have been selected for closer examination: e-commerce and the telecommunications industry.

E-commerce

Amazon.com is another early pioneer for service oriented solutions.[20] Long before the *SOA* buzzword existed, Amazon was moving toward a more loosely coupled, standards-based, and layered architectural model. The end result is a layered, transactional system that supports its one million partners and 60 million customers. Amazon.com has become a big believer in the power of service orientation, both as a technology enabler and as an organizational aligner.

eBay-owned *PayPal* has seen tremendous value in service orientation.[21] The types of tender potentially used for online payments are quite varied:

- Credit/debit
- Gift
- Loyalty programs
- Bank draft/ACH (automated clearinghouse, i.e., e-check)
- Online funds (PayPal balance)

Each tender has a unique workflow, its own security requirements, different policies and restrictions, and its own user interface. Once a retailer has overcome the hurdle of accepting payment, there is the additional challenge of integrating the various providers with its own customized protocols, data formats, and transaction semantics.[22] Service orientation is critical in order to achieve any sort of scalability.

Telecommunications

British Telecom (BT) is making a big investment in SOA in an effort to streamline business processes, consolidate legacy systems, reduce product development time, ease collaboration with partners, and improve customer value.[23] BT has a six-year SOA adoption plan:

- Consolidate 3,500 systems down to 100 (it has already eliminated nearly 1,000 as a result of SOA).
- Reduce product lifecycle across the enterprise from 18 to 6 months.
- Deliver a seamless experience to customers (single bill for multiple products, single point of contact for customer support, etc.).

BT recognizes that service orientation is more than just technology. It is tapping into SOA's ability to transform the business, changing the way people work and moving toward business metrics for measuring IT staff performance. Project success and incentives are now based on operational costs and business process efficiency. Service orientation is being used to produce a fundamental shift in the way that business gets done at BT.

Comcast, the biggest U.S. provider of cable television, cites asset reuse and quicker time to market as the primary business reasons for its SOA adoption.[24] By identifying major business processes and functionality sets, it is able to target its SOA initiative to get the most value possible. Billing, provisioning, customer service, human resources, and payroll are all a part of the company's SOA adoption plans. The billing system was one of the first to benefit from service orientation. The acquisition of AT&T Broadband resulted in its customer base being divided across two billing systems (60% in the original system, 40% in the acquired system). Before SOA, custom code had to be written using proprietary interfaces to go into each system and retrieve the necessary information. Now, a service oriented mediation layer abstracts the details of the underlying systems. The company chief information officer now boasts that new products and business processes are introduced into the enterprise in days and weeks rather than the months required in the non-SOA environment.

Dow 30 component *Verizon Communications* was formed in 2000 from the merger between GTE and Bell Atlantic, one of the largest mergers in U.S. business history. In the wake of that merger, Verizon embarked on several service orientation initiatives in order to consolidate business operations, information systems, and technology infrastructure.[25] The first initiative was to identify 500 key business functions that were used over and over again (originally duplicated across business units anywhere from 5 to 30 times across different applications). Future SOA initiatives addressed operational elements such as governance, service quality with associated service level agreements (SLAs), and scalability. When Verizon's SOA environment hit 10,000 transactions per month, the company noticed an exponential growth in its acceptance within the organization. Since then, usage has climbed to 10 million transactions per day.

TRAVEL SECTOR

Modern travel is a complex animal. Getting from point A to point B used to be fairly simple. Now it can involve any number of transportation modes, payment methods, taxes and surcharges, identification validations, luggage routing, and customs procedures. Managing the workflow and facilitating the exchange of data, security tokens, and other metadata is a ripe environment for SOA. Next we will examine three industries within the travel sector: planes, trains, and automobiles (sorry, just couldn't resist).

Planes

Stockholm-based Scandinavian *Airlines International (SAS)*, which operates 1,000 daily flights and 300 airplanes, is service orienting its enterprise in order to improve business responsiveness.[26] SAS wants to more quickly react to unexpected events like weather delays and equipment repair issues. When issues arise, as they inevitably will, you must be able to quickly reorganize your fleet plan (flights, planes, crew, gates, etc.). In addition to quicker responsiveness, SAS is projecting lower IT maintenance costs as a result of SOA to the tune of $250,000 each month.

U.S.-based *United Airlines* began its SOA effort by service enabling its mainframe systems.[27] United is now in the process of transitioning to an even more standards-based and layered architecture. The primary thrust for this SOA effort is the development of EasyFIDS, a flight information tracking system. This system provides a messaging platform with heavy emphasis on interoperability. EasyFIDS relays flight status information in real time to multiple endpoints, including airport monitors, airport personnel, flight crews, and the Federal Aviation Administration (FAA), and even directly to passengers. The system includes 22 SOA-enabled mission-critical applications that are coordinated together in the event of bad weather, airport delays, or airplane malfunction.

Trains

Railinc, a wholly owned subsidiary of the American Association of Railroads, targeted its SOA adoption to the need for a single system of record for railroad logistics.[28] Railinc's information system handles 5.8 million messages daily, coordinates with 1,500 trading partners, and tracks in excess of 7 million pieces of equipment. Data sharing and system interoperability are paramount. SOA is an obvious choice here. Railinc's leadership acknowledges that developing solutions in a service oriented way is more expensive initially, but the reuse and agility more than make up for the increase in base development costs.

Automobiles

Confronted with a saturated car rental marketplace, *Avis Rent A Car* implemented SOA to accelerate its ability to introduce new services and penetrate new markets.[29] Specifically, Avis focused on transforming its Avis.com Web presence and back-end application infrastructure into a service oriented platform. The new environment provides Avis with several key differentiators:

- Marketing campaigns can now be dynamically built, tuned, and their results accurately measured with minimal IT intervention.
- Integrating systems from partners like America West and Costco is simplified, standardized, and predictably repeatable.
- New life is breathed into older systems by including them in workflows with new components that SOA sews together, such as enabling loyalty point redemption to be built directly into the reservation workflow.

Did it work? Avis now has the highest Internet conversion rate (turning visitors into buyers) in the entire travel industry. Moreover, SOA has helped Avis improve development speed by 40%.

OnStar, the in-vehicle safety and security company owned by General Motors, is moving its technology platform to SOA to take advantage of reuse and agile business rules.[30] In order to increase operational efficiency and improve processing time, OnStar plans to remove redundant code, leverage common services, and implement a business layer. The plan is to fine-tune a smaller set of services and configurable business rules that can then be reused by multiple processes.

APPLYING SOA TO OTHER SECTORS AND SPECIFIC INDUSTRIES

If the market sector and specific industry that you are focused on has already been covered in this chapter, then you are in luck. If not, however, then you will need to identify parallels with respect to business challenges and opportunities that you can use to draw conclusions regarding SOA's applicability to your sector and industry.

The following tips can help in identifying one or more parallel case studies to get you started on the road to SOA adoption. Some of these may seem fairly obvious, others less so.

- Begin by looking for a similar business:
  - First, try to find a business in the same sector, and same or similar industry.
  - Next, try to find a business of roughly the same size in the same sector, but a different industry.
  - If you are still empty-handed, then look for a business of roughly the same size that has similar challenges but is in an entirely different market sector.
- Next, look for businesses with similar objectives:
  - Document your business drivers (i.e., time to market, cost control, agility/responsiveness, efficiency, productivity, etc.).
  - Look for businesses in your same sector and industry with similar drivers.
  - Look in other sectors and industries for businesses with similar drivers.
- Finally, look for businesses with similar challenges:
  - Document your biggest pain points (i.e., system integration, development costs, maintenance costs, inflexible architecture, scalability, etc.).
  - Look for businesses in your same sector and industry with similar issues.
  - Look in other sectors and industries for businesses with similar issues.

By now, you should have identified one or more businesses that have some similarities with your business. Now you can begin the process of examining their SOA adoption strategy, obstacles, progress, and lessons learned. Begin by following the endnotes for the case studies mentioned earlier, follow with additional research, and then consider contacting industry sources or even the firms themselves to learn more about these organizations' experiences with SOA.

SUMMARY

SOA is not a one-trick pony. It is a robust and flexible approach to addressing common challenges in enterprise architecture (EA). Service orientation is effectively being applied in the Defense, Financial, Media, Technology, and Travel sectors as well as many others. In looking at specific industry examples, common themes and motivations for service orientation emerge. Whether you find examples that directly parallel your enterprise or must go through a more detailed process to deduce which examples are applicable, there are ample examples to work with. The exciting part is that this is just the tip of the iceberg. There are hundreds of SOA case studies spread across virtually every modern industry. As you embark on your own SOA initiative, you have the good fortune of being able to learn from and take advantage of the pioneers that have gone ahead.

NOTES

1. To learn more about the DOD's information management modernization efforts, check out: www.oft.osd.mil/library/library_files/document_387_NCW_Book_LowRes.pdf.
2. For more information, consult Department of Defense Directive (DoDD) 8500.1 and Department of Defense Instruction 8500.2.
3. For more information on DOD data sharing and SOA, see www.cio.com/article/print/110100.
4. To learn more about SOA and DCGS, see www.bea.com/content/news_events/white_papers/BEA_DoD_sb.pdf.
5. Details regarding L-3 Link's AVCATT program can be found here: www.link.com/avcatt.html.
6. To read more about next-generation simulation environments, check out: www.siaa.asn.au/get/2411855829.pdf.
7. The full Synovus case study can be read here: www.active-endpoints.com/documents/documents/1/synovus-activebpel-case-study.pdf.

8. To see how SOA changed Harley-Davidson's loan processing, read: www.informationweek.com/showArticle.jhtml?articleID= 184426019.

9. To learn more about Merrill Lynch's service oriented data strategy: www.soainaction.com/blog/2007/02/merrill_lynch.php.

10. FCSAmerica's service oriented CRM is described in more detail here: http://searchsoa.techtarget.com/originalContent/0,289142, sid26_gci1241305,00.html.

11. For more information on Wachovia's SOA reuse strategy, see: www.infoworld.com/infoworld/article/06/07/13/29FEwachovia_1 .html.

12. Ameriprise used SOA to make a reuse play. Details can be found here: www.cioinsight.com/article2/0,1397,2058779,00.asp.

13. To read more about Guardian's IT cost control strategy, check out: www.infoworld.com/article/05/05/02/18FEsoaguardian_1 .html.

14. Standard Life Group saved a bundle using SOA. For the full story, go here: www.networkworld.com/techinsider/2005/101005-roi -of-soa.html.

15. To read more about how BCBS broke down silos using SOA, read: www.hoise.com/vmw/05/articles/vmw/LV-VM-12-05-12.html.

16. The full esure case study can be found here: www.bea.com/ content/news_events/white_papers/BEA_esure_cs.pdf.

17. To better understand the BBC's SOA strategy, read this: www .computing.co.uk/computing/news/2155301/bbc-lays-foundations -move-soa.

18. DreamWorks uses SOA. For details, check out: www.information week.com/management/showArticle.jhtml?articleID=181400659.

19. For the details on Sony Pictures Entertainment's use of SOA, read: www.microsoft.com/casestudies/casestudy.aspx?casestudyid=48976.

20. It's a jungle out there and Amazon has a long history of taking a service oriented approach to navigating that jungle. To learn more, read this: http://searchsoa.techtarget.com/originalContent/ 0,289142,sid26_gci1195702,00.html.

21. To learn more about how PayPal uses SOA, check out: www .javaworld.com/javaworld/jw-07-2007/jw-07-soa6.html.

22. For further details on how e-commerce companies can benefit from service orientation, read: www.ecommercetimes.com/story/ 60295.html?welcome=1199299992.

23. For more details regarding BT's big bet on SOA, check out: www.itweek.co.uk/2162201.

24. Comcast is using SOA to consolidate business and better facilitate acquisitions. To learn more, read: www.cio.com/article/121952/ Reaping_the_Big_Business_Benefits_of_SOA.
25. To better understand Verizon's tremendous investment in SOA, check out: www.infoworld.com/article/05/11/07/45FEsoacaseverizon_1 .html.
26. To read more about SAS's adoption of SOA, read: www .computerworld.com/action/article.do?command=viewArticle Basic&articleId=9018400.
27. United Airlines and the EasyFIDS system are reaping benefits from SOA. To learn more, read: www.soainaction.com/blog/2007/06/ flying_the_friendly_skies_of_s.php.
28. To learn more about Railinc's SOA-enabled master data management strategy, check out: http://searchsoa.techtarget.com/ originalContent/0,289142,sid26_gci1268947,00.html.
29. For the full Avis case study, check out: www.bea.com/content/ news_events/white_papers/BEA_Avis_cs.pdf.
30. For more details regarding OnStar's use of SOA, read: www .techweb.com/wire/software/177102037.

CHAPTER 7

CALCULATING SOA ROI

The search for technology return on investment (ROI) is an ongoing endeavor that seems to receive more or less attention depending on the success of the market and/or pressure from stockholders. Some measure of ROI is nearly always used as a justification for major technology investments within large enterprises. The veracity and level of detail for such measures, however, is suspect. Perhaps Albert Einstein said it best:

> Not everything that can be counted counts, and not everything that counts can be counted. —Albert Einstein (1879–1955)

Service oriented architecture (SOA) introduces some unique challenges in measuring ROI. SOA is an approach and a paradigm shift as much as it is a tangible technology set. Beyond XML standards for systems integration, service layering, and key infrastructure components, SOA is an agile architecture and a process-centric alignment between business and information technology (IT). All of this makes ROI calculation for SOA complex and potentially problematic. In spite of these obstacles, it is possible to construct a realistic ROI for SOA initiatives as long as you scope the project appropriately and use a service oriented ROI calculation model.

QUANTIFYING SOA ROI

Does SOA save the enterprise money? SOA introduces a mixed bag into the equation. On the one hand, service orientation represents a very ambitious undertaking that requires sweeping organizational changes, significant infrastructure investments, and broad reskilling and educational efforts. On the other hand, if the technology team is skilled and the project scope is well contained, it is actually possible to yield an almost-instantaneous ROI from service orientation.

How Fuzzy Is Your ROI?

ROI is notoriously difficult to calculate. Many speculate that it is more often measured after the fact in order to either justify or punish previous endeavors. The dirty little secret within the technology space, however, is that few enterprises employ any sort of defined process for measuring ROI. In fact, according to e-Skills, a United Kingdom–based not-for-profit organization, in their 2005 fourth-quarter ICT Inquiry report,[1] only 11% of companies calculate ROI for IT expenditures through any sort of formal methodology. The other 89% rely on "informed guesswork" or "personal intuition" for measuring the productivity returns for technology investments. *CIO Insight* conducted a similar study in 2006 and found that more than half of all executives, both IT and business executives, doubt that ROI measures used within their organizations are even accurate.

Gauging Service Oriented ROI

In a marketplace where agility is the order of the day and SOA is the latest silver bullet, ROI calculations for SOA can be particularly tricky. Adopting SOA is as much about transforming the organization and aligning business and IT as it is about exposing enterprise assets as configurable services and business processes. Combine this with the notoriously large upfront investments that most SOA infrastructures require, and it is easy to see how traditional ROI calculations can become daunting or even unrealistic in certain cases.

The value of an SOA initiative can be easily expressed in terms of soft benefits like flexibility and customer satisfaction, as well as hard benefits such as reduced total cost of ownership (TCO) and increased revenue. Most discussions of SOA ROI focus on the soft benefits of SOA as these are easier (and safer) to discuss. It is the hard, quantifiable SOA benefits that are more elusive and, consequently, the most important to explore. The quantifiable benefits of SOA can be grouped into three categories:

1. **Short-term tactical ROI.** Easily quantifiable on a project-specific basis by measuring the reduction in integration expenses required.
2. **Medium-term operational ROI.** Tougher to quantify; savings is derived through reuse of enterprise assets.
3. **Long-term strategic ROI.** Difficult to quantify; savings and increased revenue are based on agility afforded through service infrastructure and business alignment.

We will explore each of these categories in turn. In some cases, formal ROI calculation models exist; in other cases, there are simply some solid guidelines and best practices to employ.

TACTICAL SOA ROI

In the short term, SOA initiatives can yield immediate, tactical ROI in the form of cost reductions. Primarily, these cost savings are realized in the form of reducing (or in some cases eliminating) middleware licensing fees, reduced development time, and lower costs for system maintenance and system configuration.

Understanding Tactical SOA ROI

There are two primary drivers behind tactical SOA ROI. First, SOA enables enterprises to reduce or even eliminate redundant functionality and integration mechanisms. Capabilities can be consolidated, or in some cases centralized, reducing licensing and corresponding maintenance costs.

The second tactical ROI driver focuses upon standards-based integration techniques rather than proprietary interfaces and protocols. This allows integration solutions to be provided without the need for costly vendor-specific and/or platform-specific conduits. This opens up the systems integration landscape and allows for less expensive (or even free) software to be utilized. Furthermore, this keeps staff training costs low due to the use of well-known standard protocols and messaging formats.

Computing Tactical ROI

Computing tactical ROI is simple and straightforward. Results and projections are based on project-specific savings that are realized via SOA. No formal cost models exist for tactical ROI calculation; you just need to clearly define the project scope, the initial investment, and the short-term financial objectives, and then use a good spreadsheet, calculator, or abacus to compute the tactical value for the SOA initiative. The steps are:

1. Compute the savings realized due to reduced middleware licensing costs.
2. Compute the savings afforded due to reduced development time.
3. If you are leveraging services from a third party or reusing services from another project, then you can project savings due to reduced maintenance and development costs versus developing capabilities from scratch.
4. Add together the results of steps 1 through 3 and fold that into whatever ROI formula your organization uses (e.g., net gain divided by investment).

Tactical ROI is typically used to justify an initial SOA pilot project or as a way to reduce financial risk associated with a particular SOA initiative. For broad adoption of SOA, tactical ROI alone is not sufficient. In order to provide more significant value, businesses must look toward *operational ROI*.

OPERATIONAL SOA ROI

Whereas tactical ROI focuses on quick wins, operational ROI aims more at generating value through reuse of capabilities and services over time. In the short-to-medium time frame, SOA can provide an ROI in the form of supporting day-to-day operations through enterprise asset reuse. Enterprise reuse has really taken center stage with many Fortune 500 companies as a key way to reduce development and maintenance costs and speed time to market. Through the use of standard protocols and messaging formats as well as loosely coupled interfaces, service and business process reuse has been given real momentum by SOA.

Understanding Operational ROI

Case studies and industry research reveal some pretty startling efficiencies available through reuse. Developing a solution by reusing existing components and business rules can reduce costs by as much as 75% (though most metrics peg the number closer to 20%). Maintenance cost savings are even more significant, with some research identifying a 5 times or even 10 times savings factor.[2]

The key is to identify areas of commonality between legacy systems and build common services and/or processes. These common services may be developed locally or provided via a third party such as the government, a business partner, or a service vendor. Common services may be developed for a particular line of business or may support an entire enterprise. Christopher Crowhurst, Vice President and principal architect at Thomson Learning, described the importance of service oriented reuse when he told *Network World* in an October 2005 article entitled "The ROI of SOA":[3]

I can guarantee there's a cheaper way to build your next product, but there's no cheaper way to build your next 20 products [than SOA]. —*Christopher Crowhurst, VP and principal architect at Thomson Learning*

There are a couple of cost models available for calculating SOA operational ROI:

1. **Iterative reuse model.** Investment return is measured based on number of times a service or process is reused rather than an arbitrary time frame
2. **Calculated reuse model.** This mathematical model computes SOA value based on a few key variables such as number of services available for reuse, degree of reuse, and service complexity.

Computing Operational ROI: Iterative Reuse Model

The *iterative reuse model* works off the premise that although the initial investment in reusable services is expensive, an ROI can be achieved based on reuse. The savings achieved through reuse of existing assets versus creating capabilities from scratch each time eventually outweigh the added initial investment. To understand this better, we need to introduce some data points:

- **The initial investment in developing reusable enterprise assets is significant.** It turns out that developing something so that it is able to solve current requirements and also has the capacity to be reused in other situations is not free. In fact, industry expert Dr. Jeffrey Poulin estimates an increased cost of 60% on average (with some estimates ranging as high as 300%) for initial development of reusable components rather than single-use components.[4]
- **Consuming existing services/processes reduces development costs.** If an existing service is available that already meets some or all of your requirements, then your solution development costs can be dramatically reduced. Dr. Poulin estimates that leveraging an

existing component is 80% cheaper (with data ranging from 0% to 100%) than developing that same capability from scratch.

- **As these reusable enterprise assets are leveraged in later projects, an ROI emerges.** While the initial investment in developing services so that they have a high potential for reuse requires additional upfront costs, a return on that investment occurs over time. ROI can be realized as early as the first instance of reuse, but is typically realized on the second or third instance of reuse.

Taking these figures and applying them to a nominal scenario where a particular capability is required for an information system, we can better understand the economics of reuse. For the purposes of illustration, we will assume that a project needs an authentication capability as a part of an internal Web application. We propose developing this capability as a service that can be reused for future projects that have the same or similar requirements. Assuming the base of cost of developing this authentication service is $10,000, we can see the power of reuse as illustrated in Exhibit 7.1.

The simple example illustrated in Exhibit 7.1 is a bit idealistic, however, indicating that an ROI could be seen as early as the first instance of reuse. Your results are likely to differ. A variety of factors come into play, including excessive upfront costs for making services reusable (many practitioners claim a two times cost factor at development time), added development costs in order to refactor services that are almost

EXHIBIT **7.1** *The iterative reuse model measures value based on the number of times a service is reused*

	Base Cost	Reuse Impact	Project Cost	Running Cost	Return On Investment
Initial Development	$10,000	+60%	$16,000	$16,000	−$6,000
First Reuse	$10,000	−80%	$2,000	$18,000	$2,000
Second Reuse	$10,000	−80%	$2,000	$20,000	$10,000
Third Reuse	$10,000	−80%	$2,000	$22,000	$18,000

reusable, and additional costs due to lack of team skills and experience in SOA. Perhaps even more important, in reality, an ROI tends to emerge around the second or third instance of reuse.

Computing Operational ROI: Calculated Reuse Model

The *calculated reuse model*[5] aims to compute the value of an SOA initiative based on a few key data points, including initial service development cost, cost per operation, the number of reusable services, service complexity, and a reusability factor. Successful use of this model requires an established cost baseline for your non-SOA development. You will need some metrics on current development costs (per function, per object point, per line of code, etc.) so that you can compare those against the costs associated with service oriented reuse.

This model uses a mathematical formula to determine reuse-based ROI. To start with, we will define the variables involved in that formula:

- **Service development cost (SDC).** This is the cost associated with initial development of services.
- **Cost per function (CPF).** This means development cost per function, object point, or line of code.
- **Number of reusable services (NRS).** These are services created or leveraged.
- **Service complexity factor (SCF).** This is the average number of functions or object points within each service.
- **Degree of reuse (DR).** This is the percentage reflecting the number of times services are reused out of possible usage scenarios and/or the percentage of operations reused.

These variables are then folded into the following formula:

$$SDC - NRS * DR * SCF * CPF = ROI$$

If you expand the acronyms, then the formula reads as follows:

Development cost − Number of services ∗ Reuse percentage
    ∗ Number of functions/object points/lines of code
    ∗ Cost per function/object/line
    = Return on investment

To see this in action, we will look at one negative ROI example and then two positive ROI examples:

Negative ROI Example: $50,000 − 50 ∗ .4 ∗ 200 ∗ $10.00
= −$10,000 ROI

Positive ROI Example 1: $50,000 − 75 ∗ .4 ∗ 200 ∗ $10.00
= +$10,000 ROI (more services)

Positive ROI Example 2: $50,000 − 50 ∗ .6 ∗ 200 ∗ $10.00
= +$10,000 ROI (increased reuse)

As these examples illustrate, an initial development cost of $50,000 that involves 50 services, with a 40% reuse rate, 200 lines of code (LOC), and a development cost of $10/LOC, will result in a negative ROI. However, by increasing the number of services to 75 or by increasing the degree of reuse that is achieved from the original 50 services, then a positive ROI emerges. This underscores just how interconnected the variables are in this formula.

Regardless of which model is used, operational ROI is realized in terms of service and process reuse. While operational ROI offers tremendous value, in order to reap the full potential of SOA, an even more ambitious investment will need to be made. This is where *strategic ROI* comes into play.

Heavier initial investments are needed to develop reusable enterprise services, but over time, across multiple projects and instances of reuse, an ROI emerges.

STRATEGIC SOA ROI

In the medium-to-long-term time frame, there is a more strategic ROI made available via business agility. Strategic ROI is manifested through cost controls, risk mitigation, and new revenue generation as a result of agility.

Understanding Strategic ROI

Strategic ROI is the ultimate expression of what SOA is all about. It is about making a strategic investment in an agile enterprise infrastructure and at the same time aligning the business and technology sides of the organization to work toward common, shared objectives. Rather than viewing IT as a cost of doing business, it becomes a strategic partner that enables the organization to effectively and efficiently manage information and capture new business by making the enterprise nimble and more responsive to opportunities and risks. An agile architecture provides cost savings in development and maintenance and risk mitigation in the form of improved regulatory compliance (e.g., Health Insurance Portability and Accountability Act [HIPAA], Sarbanes-Oxley, etc.). Agility also serves as a revenue driver, by enabling the rapid creation of new products and services to meet changing client and market demands.

Computing Strategic ROI

Similar to tactical ROI calculation, no real cost models exist for calculating strategic ROI. There are, however, some key elements to consider:

- System development and maintenance costs are saved due to the ability to modify information systems with little or no coding required (simply modify or rearrange the orchestration of several services).
- Estimated legal costs and fines are avoided due to faster and more reliable responsiveness to regulatory changes.

- Revenue is generated via the rapid creation of new services as well as the manipulation and reconfiguration of existing ones.
- Revenue is generated due to ability to expose internal capabilities as consumable services by business partners and clients (this potentially generates completely new streams of income).

The potential return on agility is tremendous. The ability to strategically position the enterprise to gain first-mover advantage, capitalize on market opportunities, and adapt to changing environmental factors is invaluable. Calculating strategic ROI is fuzzy and prone to significant margins for error. The elements previously outlined are provided as a guide, but many organizations choose to make a strategic investment in SOA to gain agility without hard numbers to quantify this move. The return on strategic SOA is just too huge for enterprises to ignore.

SCHEDULE AND RISK: THE HIDDEN FACTORS IN EVALUATING ROI

Up to now, we have examined three ROI categories (tactical, operational, and strategic) in a vacuum. In reality, the decision regarding which ROI calculation approach is right for your business will be largely determined based on two factors that drive many decisions from behind the scenes: schedule and risk.

Two important considerations when evaluating ROI are the time frame for investment return (schedule) and the sponsor's tolerance for delay, complications, and potential cost overruns (risk). The three ROI categories outlined earlier are typically realized in three very different time frames with escalating potential for both risk and reward. Exhibit 7.2 illustrates the spectrum of possibilities.

To some degree, Exhibit 7.2 begs the question of exactly what constitutes short, medium, and long time frames. The reality is that this will vary depending on the size of the SOA initiative. For a relatively small SOA deployment, a short-term time frame might be two months and a long-term time frame might be nine months. For a more substantial

EXHIBIT 7.2   *Each of the three ROI categories is bound to a different time frame and bears escalating risk*

ROI Type	Time Frame	Associated Risk	Potential Return
Tactical	immediate to short	low	minor net gain
Operational	short to medium or based on instances of reuse	low to moderate	significant return beyond 2nd or 3rd instance of reuse
Strategic	medium to long	moderate to high	risk reduction and lucrative revenue driver

SOA deployment, we might talk in terms of six months for short and three to five years for long. Also keep in mind that when viewing the operational ROI time frame, we may even throw out an arbitrary timeline and instead think in terms of achieving an ROI after a certain number of reuse instances.

CASE STUDY: CALCULATING SOA ROI

Taking a look at our Return Handling and Expense Approval case studies outlined earlier, we can better understand how SOA ROI calculations operate within a real-world context. Up to this point, we do not have sufficient information from either case study to actually make an ROI calculation. As such, we will introduce additional details with each respective case study.

SOA ROI for the *Return Handling* Case Study

For our mail-order company, we will examine SOA ROI from a tactical perspective. After conducting a feasibility study, our project team was able to identify the following data points that are relevant to tactical ROI:

- IT spends $143,000 per year in middleware license maintenance fees, $68,000 of which is used to connect the various systems that

EXHIBIT **7.3**   *Tactical ROI calculation for the Return Handling case*

Annual Maintenance Savings (15 hrs × $72/hr × 12 mos)	$ 12,960
Annual License Fee Savings	$ 68,000
Annual Savings	$ 80,960
Project Development Costs (one-time fee)	−$ 45,000
First Year Savings	$ 35,960

currently support handling of customer returns. Initial proof-of-concept work indicates that this $68,000 annual expense can be avoided by using standard service interfaces.

- Based on industry data, the SOA pilot project deployed last year, and initial estimates by the project management team, it is believed that integrating these systems via standard, service-based interfaces and messaging protocols will yield a reduction in time spent maintaining the system by 15 hours per month.
- The cost of system maintenance resources is $72 per hour.
- The project management team estimates that this portion of the SOA initiative will cost $45,000 to implement.

So how does our tactical ROI analysis work out? According to Exhibit 7.3, there will be a first-year savings of nearly $36,000 and an annual savings of over $80,000 for each subsequent year—not too shabby.

SOA ROI for the *Expense Approval* Case Study

Next we will take a look at our Expense Approval case study. We will examine this one from a reuse perspective (i.e., operational ROI). After conducting a feasibility study, our project team was able to identify the following data points that are relevant for calculating operational ROI (we will use the calculated reuse model):

- Service orienting the systems that comprise the expense approval process will incur a base cost of $60,000 (five services with an average cost of $12,000 each). The team plans to incur additional cost of $30,000 to make those services reusable (base cost × .60).

- Three of those services are expected to be reused twice within the next 18 months, yielding a projected savings of $57,600 ([3 services × $12,000 base] = $36,000, [$36,000 × 0.8 savings for reuse] = $28,800, [$28,800 × two instances of reuse = $57,600]).

So how does our SOA ROI calculation work out? Our initial development costs total $90,000 ($60,000 base plus $30,000 to make the services reusable). According to our project team's projections, there is a savings potential of only $57,600. That leaves us short over $30,000 to merely break even. It looks as though service orientation does not make sense for HighTree, at least not according to the calculated reuse model.

SUMMARY

Once you get past the hype surrounding SOA and take a close look at it, there is significant, practical value for organizations to capitalize on. Moreover, this value is tangible, and a definable ROI for SOA can actually be determined. The calculation of SOA ROI is still fairly immature. In time, we will no doubt have more comprehensive models for calculating and measuring the value of an SOA initiative. For now, we have some solid guidelines for short-term (tactical) and long-term (strategic) SOA ROI and two ROI calculation models that have emerged in the middle (operational).

SOA adoption does not need to be approached blindly. Clients, investors, and sponsors expect tangible data on which to base investment decisions. SOA should be no exception. An ROI for SOA initiatives can be provided and a roadmap for SOA adoption can be undertaken using incremental, measured steps.

> SOA can align and transform your organization and you do not have to harvest your internal organs or lease your office as a bingo parlor on the weekend in order to pay for it.

NOTES

1. To read the full report from e-Skills, check out: www.e-skills.com/cgi-bin/orad.pl/358/ictinquiry_5_q4_2005.pdf.
2. For more details regarding reuse metrics, read: *Software Reuse: Architecture, Process, and Organization for Business Success*, by Jacobson, Griss, and Jonsson, ACM Press, 1997; and also: "Predictable Software: Order Out of Chaos," by Paige, June 1994 (CrossTalk); and also: "Once Is Not Enough," Hunter, 1997 (*CIO* magazine).
3. To read more about SOA ROI, check out: www.networkworld.com/techinsider/2005/101005-roi-of-soa.html.
4. For additional details on software reuse metrics, read: Jeffrey S. Poulin, *Measuring Software Reuse: Principles, Practices, and Economic Models*, Addison-Wesley, Reading, MA, 1997.
5. The "calculated reuse model" is based on research and analysis conducted by David Linthicum and expressed in "The ROI of Your SOA," by David Linthicum, www.ebizq.net/topics/soa/features/6092.html.

HOW SHOULD I GO ABOUT ADOPTING SOA?

With a better understanding of service oriented architecture (SOA) and a clearer vision regarding its applicability for your business, you are better equipped to pursue SOA adoption. This part of the book addresses the subject of how to adopt SOA where it makes sense, in a way that is measurable and low risk and is actually accepted by the organization. A comprehensive SOA evaluation and adoption strategy is provided in the final chapter.

Chapter 8, "Selecting an SOA Maturity Model," introduces the subject of maturity modeling and the motivations behind it (both proactive and reactive). Three specific models are introduced and thoroughly examined. Finally, best practice guidance is given regarding selecting a model that is right for your business.

Chapter 9, "How Much SOA Do I Need?," begins by highlighting the fallacy of using SOA to solve every IT challenge. This chapter illustrates the importance of striking a balance in how and to what extent SOA is used within the enterprise. It then introduces the Selective SOA™ methodology, which facilitates the identification of enterprise business systems and processes that are optimal for service orientation (applying the 20/80 rule).

Chapter 10, "Acquiring the Skills for SOA," highlights the importance of education when adopting SOA. Education supports the acquisition of new skills and transition of existing skills. Skill development is essential for successful adoption of SOA. Mindset-shifting is equally important. Service orientation requires teams and individuals to approach problems differently and apply different patterns to solve them. Education is critical to this process.

Chapter 11, "Risk Mitigation through Proper Governance," introduces and defines governance (it turns out to be a lot like bowling) and its purpose in SOA adoption and ongoing success. The absence of governance is described through three touch points (providing a service, consuming a service, supporting agreements) and three manifestations of governance (procedures, policies, metrics) are described. The bulk of the chapter details ten steps to successful SOA governance.

Chapter 12, "Creating Your SOA Adoption Plan," describes how to put a definitive plan in place. Now that you are armed with the knowledge of SOA, its ups and downs, and strategies for adopting it, this chapter outlines a six-step plan that moves from SOA evaluation (identify business drivers, pilot project, and strategic analysis) to SOA adoption (crystallize requirements, define adoption plan, and communicate SOA across the organization).

CHAPTER 8

SELECTING AN SOA MATURITY MODEL

As children, we are enamored with the concept of *maturity*. We look forward to each new phase of life with great anticipation (and corresponding fear on the part of our parents). Children are very interested in proving that they are "big" (a phenomenally relative concept) and are quite interested in gauging this growth. My child is not merely four; he is four and *a half!* Equally important to children is the dualistic practice of identifying those peers who are *not* mature or "big." Hence the childhood quip: "Act your age, not your shoe size."

In the business world, gauging the growth or relative maturity of enterprises is sought in the form of formal models. These maturity models are sometimes applied to whole industries or uniquely crafted for use within a given organization. Perhaps the most well-known is the Capability Maturity Model Integrated (CMMI) developed by the Software Engineering Institute (SEI). The strategic utilization of service oriented architecture (SOA) within enterprises and the sheer scale of many SOA initiatives warrant a disciplined and measured approach to adopting SOA. To address this need, several SOA maturity models have emerged. These models are then utilized to gauge the relative maturity of an enterprise's SOA adoption or even to gauge the maturity of a more comprehensive enterprise architecture (EA) strategy. Is it any wonder that some are saying that organizations should now "act their age, not their SOA size?"

GAUGING MATURITY

Organizations gauge the maturity of their EA/SOA adoption for one of two fundamental reasons:

1. *Reactive* benchmarking to determine where the organization is with respect to other business units or enterprises
2. *Proactive* strategy and planning to align EA/SOA initiatives with objective criteria and business goals

Inevitably, gauging the organization's maturity leads to the examination of formal maturity models. The reactive/proactive perspectives do not materially change the crafting or populating of the models; they simply change the metrics, reporting, and interpretation of them. Generally, either the available models are standalone, SOA-specific models or they depend on and define a mapping to CMMI (which is great if you are working with an organization that is familiar with this approach).

SOA MATURITY MODELS AT A GLANCE

The vast majority of SOA maturity models borrow concepts and even terminology from the battle-tested Capability Maturity Model (CMM) and its successor, the CMMI, both developed by SEI. SEI's maturity models have been used for years to evaluate and measure software maturity and integration processes according to a tiered set of maturity levels.

SOA maturity models tend to borrow liberally from SEI's CMM and CMMI models.[1] They borrow the concept of tiered maturity levels and will even frequently borrow the terminology and progression levels. The difference is that SEI's maturity models are intended to gauge the maturity of an organization's *processes*. SOA maturity models typically attempt to gauge the maturity of *architecture* (although the best models measure both).

An extensive list of SOA maturity models could be compiled based on a few good Google[TM] queries. Many of these models either are company specific or have been espoused by various SOA experts in the form of blog and/or forum posts. There are, however, three models that have been formally defined and repeatedly applied to yield successful SOA results for enterprise organizations:

1. **Web Services Maturity Model** by CBDI Forum
2. **Service Integration Maturity Model** (SIMM) by IBM
3. **Service Oriented Architecture Maturity Model** (SOA MM) by Progress-Sonic Software and a consortium of other vendors

We will start by introducing each model and highlighting its essential structure and core concepts. Later we will identify some useful guidelines for selecting the right SOA maturity model for your organization.

WEB SERVICES MATURITY MODEL[2]

United Kingdom–based CBDI Forum promotes the oldest service maturity model (circa 2003) of the bunch. CBDI defines a business and technology maturity model that centers on *Web Services* as the dominate technology components within an SOA infrastructure.

Model Basics

Given its legacy, the model assumes XML-based Web Services as a key technology enabler for SOA. These services and the corresponding infrastructure are matured and enhanced in phases. Within each phase, technology and organizational implications are addressed. The model defines four major phases that organizations move through in the process of transitioning to a service oriented environment:

1. **Early learning.** Focus is on *technology services* and better application integration.
2. **Integration.** Focus is on *business drivers*, process modeling, and service orchestration.

3. **Reengineering.** Focus is on *measuring and monitoring* SOA and organizational transformation.
4. **Maturity.** Service ubiquity, federation, and collaboration exist within a *customer-centric and process-driven environment*.

The model goes on to discuss timelines, custom roadmaps, and best practices for applying these phases.

Model Details

To better understand the model, each phase will be described in greater detail followed by an examination of CBDI's service model.

The *early learning* phase is an exploratory phase in which the focus is on technology services and better application integration. Activity is largely directed internally as existing systems are adorned with service wrappers. This approach is often described as a *botttom-up* approach to service orientation. The idea is that you start with the bottom layer (your existing infrastructure) and develop your SOA by exposing these existing assets as standards-based and potentially re-usable services.

The second phase, *integration*, introduces a focus on business drivers. Business process modeling and service orchestration emerge in order to facilitate an alignment with business objectives. This begins to incorporate elements of a more *top-down* approach to service orientation in which business drivers and business processes frame the requirements for SOA. From a technology perspective, services become increasingly sophisticated during this phase by applying security and reliability controls. Finally, external-facing services are deployed for the first time, broadening the scope of the overall SOA initiative.

Building on the previous two phases, *reengineering* seeks to fine tune the business climate and supporting technology infrastructure. This phase applies measuring and monitoring activities and corresponding infrastructure to produce enterprise-class services. Additionally, service orientation becomes embedded in the fiber of the enterprise, impacting organizational responsibilities, funding decisions, and even product development life cycles. Further expanding the scope of SOA, increasing attention is given during this third phase to providing and consuming external services with trusted partners.

The final phase, *maturity*, is fairly ambitious and idealistic, a trap into which many of the maturity models tend to fall. This phase is characterized by ubiquitous services that function as a part of federated, collaborative service exchanges. Solutions are most often assembled from existing service and process assets and very little new capabilities are developed. Moreover, services are finally customer-centric and process-driven rather than company-centric.

Although both technology maturity and business maturity are discussed in the model, the emphasis in CBDI's model is clearly on the progressive evolution of the service technology. Exhibit 8.1 illustrates this service model. Throughout each phase, services evolve with respect to one of five indicators (drivers, service perspective, service deployments, collaborations, and service process). Over time, services become more flexible, more business-oriented, more customer-centric, and more aligned with organizational processes.

EXHIBIT **8.1**   *CBDI's maturity model consists of four progressive phases*

Drivers	*Technical*	*Business*	*Enterprise*	*Industry/ Ecosystem*
Service Perspective	Technical Interface	Business Capability	Business Product	Domain Standard
Service Deployments	Integrated	Architected	Measured and Managed	Federated
Collaborations	Internal	Limited External	Virtual Business	Anonymous
Service Process	Momentum	Extended Momentum	Reengineered	Standardized
	Early Learning	**Integration**	**Reengineering**	**Maturity**

Applying This Model

Although this model has been around the longest and takes a very intuitive approach to SOA maturity, it seems a bit fluffy in certain places. It has the right concept of progression, throws around obligatory buzzwords, and attempts to address both the technology and business aspects of SOA (there are many SOA maturity models out there that focus entirely on service technology). However, the model seems to be fairly generic, lacking the level of detail provided by some of the other SOA maturity models discussed later. Additionally, the final phase, *maturity*, appears to be tossed out there half-heartedly and with very little thought to what it actually entails.

Organizations that choose to use this model must take care to flesh out the details that the model does not initially address. Specifics must be defined regarding the progression of SOA infrastructure, not just the services themselves. Details must also be mapped out regarding technology standards, organizational change, and, most importantly, governance. CBDI's model offers a very good framework for gauging and tracking the maturing of Web Services and aligning them with business drivers and processes. With some additional details hammered out and a solid governance plan in place, this maturity model can serve to effectively enable the adoption of SOA within the enterprise.

SERVICE INTEGRATION MATURITY MODEL[3]

IBM, one of the foremost authorities on SOA, defines the Service Integration Maturity Model (SIMM). SIMM aims to facilitate business flexibility through SOA adoption while minimizing risk. IBM's SIMM is squarely focused on technology maturity and service complexity.

Model Basics

IBM's model involves the gradual application of *seven levels of SOA maturity:*

Level 1: Silo (data integration). Characterized by brittle, ad-hoc integration solutions that do not adapt well to change.

Level 2: Integrated (application integration). Applications are integrated using proprietary connections and platform-specific technologies as a part of an *enterprise application integration (EAI)* infrastructure.

Level 3: Componentized (functional integration). Modularization of significant and/or critical applications occurs. Integration efforts are typically based on well-defined interfaces (contract-driven design).

Level 4: Simple services (process integration). Initial seeds of SOA are planted in the form of individual, atomic services.

Level 5: Composite services (supply-chain integration). Value chains are constructed to form a service ecosystem for on-demand interaction among suppliers, consumers, and brokers.

Level 6: Virtualized services (virtual infrastructure). Pervasive decoupling of enterprise resources results in the development of a *virtualized service grid*. Quality-of-service monitoring and management are also externalized through an event-driven architecture.

Level 7: Dynamically reconfigurable services (ecosystem integration). Runtime composition and configuration of services is enabled via externalized policy descriptions and business process logic.

The model goes on to discuss strategies and shortcomings associated with mapping SIMM to CMMI. Mapping to CMMI levels, integration capabilities, and associated practices are discussed. Finally, IBM recommends an incremental SOA adoption planning process and the development of custom roadmaps.

Model Details

IBM's SIMM methodology defines seven levels of maturity from *silo* all the way to *dynamically reconfigurable services*. Across each level, there are seven facets that are evaluated:

1. **Business view.** How does the business view information technology (IT) solutions? (Business initially views IT from a functional perspective and eventually shifts to a service oriented view as the enterprise matures.)
2. **Organization.** Where is the IT organization focusing its efforts and activities? (This varies from application-specific skills, to governance, to technology adoption, and beyond.)
3. **Methods.** What predominant methodologies is the IT organization employing to create solutions? (Examples include structured, object oriented, and service oriented.)
4. **Applications.** How are applications composed? (Examples include modules, objects, components, services, and processes.)
5. **Architecture.** What is the overriding architectural approach? (Examples include layered, component, and SOA.)
6. **Information.** How is information accessed and made available within the enterprise? (This tends to be a description of how standardized and readily sharable data is within the enterprise.)
7. **Infrastructure.** How standardized and loosely coupled is the supporting technology infrastructure? (Initially, this is platform specific and it transforms over time to become more loosely coupled and technology agnostic.)

This produces a matrix like the one depicted in Exhibit 8.2. In the following paragraphs, we will briefly survey these 49 data points and attempt to identify trends and major themes regarding SIMM.

Level one, *silo*, describes those organizations that are still heavily employing proprietary, ad-hoc, and largely data-centric integration strategies. The business views solutions in terms of discrete functions. These solutions are supported by application-specific and vendor-specific skillsets, and the overall architecture and set of business capabilities is constrained by legacy decisions regarding platforms, vendors, databases, and software packages.

EXHIBIT 8.2   IBM's SIMM defines seven levels of maturity and seven facets at each level

	Silo	Integrated	Componentized	Services	Composite Services	Virtualized Services	Dynamically Configurable Services
Business View	Function Oriented	Function Oriented	Function Oriented	Service Oriented	Service Oriented	Service Oriented	Service Oriented
Organization	Application-Specific Skills	IT Transformation	IT Governance	Technology Adoption	Organizational Transformation	Cultural & Behavioural Transformation	Human Service Bus
Methods	Structured Analysis & Design	Object-Oriented Modeling	Component-Based Development	Service Oriented Modeling	Service Oriented Modeling	Service Oriented Modeling	Grammar-Oriented Modeling
Applications	Modules	Objects	Components	Services	Process Integration via Services	Process Integration via Services	Dynamic Application Assembly
Architecture	Monolithic Architecture	Layered Architecture	Component Architecture	Emerging SOA	SOA	Grid-Enabled SOA	Dynamically Reconfigurable Architecture
Information	Application-Specific Data Solution	Data Subject Areas Established	Business Data Can Be Shared Outside the Silo	LOB-wide Standardized Data Vocabularies	Enterprise-wide Standardized Data Vocabularies	Flexible Data Vocabularies for Expansion	Data Vocabularies Are Standards Based
Infrastructure	Platform Specific	Platform Specific	Platform Specific	Platform Specific	Platform Independent	Technology Neutral	Dynamic Sense & Respond
	Level 1	Level 2	Level 3	Level 4	Level 5	Level 6	Level 7

The second level, *integrated*, indicates a move toward object-oriented technologies and a more layered architecture. A more comprehensive integration strategy emerges, typically employing some sort of EAI platform. IT's flexibility as well as the business capabilities made available to the enterprise are still limited, but progress is being made.

A component-oriented model emerges in the third level of maturity, *componentized*. Although the business still views IT from a function-oriented perspective, business data is now shareable outside of arbitrary silos, time to market is improving through a component architecture, and maintenance costs are lowering due to component-based solutions. Additionally, the notion of IT governance tends to emerge and begins to take root at this level, representing a significant milestone with respect to the IT organization's maturity.

Simple services, the fourth maturity level, finally introduces the first sign of SOA. Common vocabularies emerge within business units, the business begins viewing IT differently (service oriented rather than function oriented), and solution development evolves to become service oriented and model driven. This level tends to produce more rapid time to market and further-reduced maintenance costs.

SOA really begins to take root during *composite services*, the fifth level of SIMM. Enterprise-wide vocabularies emerge, services are orchestrated into processes, and the IT organization transforms to become more oriented around services and processes. Additionally, standardization becomes more widespread, moving the technology infrastructure to a platform-neutral model. Significant improvements in IT efficiency, productivity, and flexibility are typically realized at this stage of the game.

The sixth level, *virtualized services*, indicates a shift toward more flexible and pervasive service orientation. Data vocabularies are flexible, SOA is delivered via an on-demand capability grid, and the infrastructure moves from being platform independent to even being technology independent.

The final level, *dynamically reconfigurable services*, represents a quantum shift in terms of strategic business alignment. Solutions can be dynamically assembled and modified to adapt to changing business needs. Infrastructure tools and governance processes are proactive rather than reactive. Solutions are modeled grammatically to match business processes through the use of a human service bus. If that sounds like a bunch of hogwash, you are not alone. The seventh level of SIMM describes the IT equivalent of *Maslow's self-actualization*. According to Maslow, only a handful of people have ever achieved self-actualization. Likewise, only a few companies (if any) will ever achieve this level of ultimate maturity and harmony. In all likelihood, by the time they do, the game will have changed and the business world will have moved toward an entirely new methodology.

Applying This Model

SIMM defines a very thorough progression of technology capabilities. It is the only model that really describes how enterprises evolve from early data-integration efforts, into EAI, and eventually into SOA. Other models tend to assume that your first level of maturity already includes services. The SIMM model provides a detailed analysis of how the evolution of SOA truly occurs. Enterprises that are taking a fairly IT-centric approach to SOA or those that already heavily leverage IBM solutions will tend to get the most out of SIMM.

Organizations that choose to use this model must take care to flesh out the details that the model does not fully explore. The model comes short in terms of how SOA impacts the organization. Lip service is given to business benefits and an organizationally focused adoption strategy, but very little attention is given to these important subjects. As with the CBDI model explored earlier, details must also be mapped out regarding technology standards, organizational change, and, most importantly, governance. IBM's model offers a very good framework for gauging and tracking the maturing of technology infrastructure, architecture, and services. With some additional details hammered out and a solid governance plan in place, this maturity model can serve to effectively enable the adoption of SOA within the enterprise.

SERVICE ORIENTED ARCHITECTURE MATURITY MODEL[4]

A consortium of vendors led by Progress-Sonic Software has developed the SOA MM, which is explicitly based on CMMI. SOA MM aims to provide IT decision makers with "a simple framework for benchmarking the strategic value of their SOA implementation, and a model for visualizing future success."

Model Basics

Modeling itself after CMMI's maturity levels, SOA MM defines five levels of maturity with respect to SOA adoption. At each level, the model identifies progressive business benefits that the organization will be able to realize. As Exhibit 8.3 illustrates, the five maturity levels and key business impacts are:

EXHIBIT **8.3**   *Progress-Sonic's SOA MM defines five levels of maturity, modeled after the CMMI*

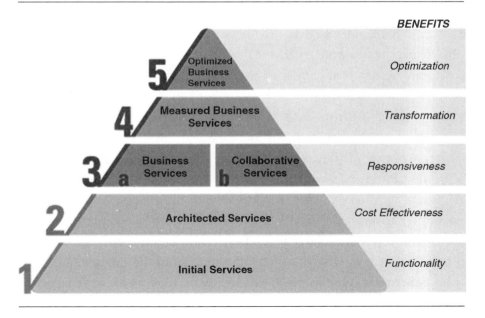

Level 1: Initial services (functionality). Deploy simple services as a part of research and development and/or pilot projects. Also define initial ROI measurement criteria and define organizational needs for SOA.

Level 2: Architected services (cost effectiveness). Design and implement an SOA infrastructure based on standards and planned reuse. Establish architectural leadership and identify SOA informational needs of the organization.

Level 3: Business and collaborative services (responsiveness). Establish SOA governance, service life cycle policies, and cross-organizational partnerships. Move toward process-centric solutions and engage business and IT in the definition, modeling, and ownership of business processes.

Level 4: Measured business services (transformation). Transform the organization from a reactive approach to solving business problems to a real-time, process-centric business. Establish service performance criteria and associated monitoring infrastructure.

Level 5: Optimized business services (optimization). Continuously improve and refine the organization and associated technology infrastructure. Proactively address business needs and facilitate future strategic initiatives.

In addition to identifying the maturity of SOA adoption and the associated business benefits, the model also maps *scope, technical success factors, organization success factors, relevant standards, key goals*, and *key practices* at each maturity level.

Model Details

Within each level of SOA MM, several business and technology facets are examined.[5] This model examines the following factors:

- **Prime business benefits.** What value proposition justifies this level of maturity to the business? (Examples include IT cost reduction and business responsiveness.)

- **Scope.** To what extent has SOA embedded itself within the enterprise? (Examples include pilot project, integrated applications, business processes, and cross-enterprise.)
- **Critical technology success factors.** What technology capabilities must the organization realize or challenges must the organization overcome in order to succeed at a given level of maturity? (Examples include legacy integration, reliable messaging, and cross-enterprise security.)
- **Critical business success factors.** What degree of support/sponsorship must the organization achieve or people challenges must the organization overcome in order to succeed at a given level of maturity? (Examples include chief information officer [CIO] sponsorship and business unit sponsorship, also governance, skills development, and a culture of continuous improvement.)
- **Selected relevant standards.** Which standards become potentially relevant at each level of maturity? (Examples include XML, SOAP, WSDL, WS-Policy, ebXML, and WS-BPEL.)
- **Key goals.** What milestones are in place at each level of maturity? (Examples include defining initial ROI measurements, establishing architecture leadership, extending SOA business processes to external organizations, and proving returns from reuse.)
- **Key practices.** What activities are essential at each level of maturity? (Examples include creating service definitions, specifying technology standards, providing organization-wide training, specifying policies, and implementing ongoing business process evaluation and reengineering.)

Initial services, the first level of SOA MM, is really designed to be the pilot phase of SOA adoption. Critical factors here include selecting technology standards, integrating legacy systems, getting some initial sponsorship, and developing new skills. All the basic standards come into play here, including XML, XSLT, SOAP, and WSDL. In addition to the learning process, initial metrics are gathered here regarding the cost and time involved in developing and deploying SOA solutions.

From this, preliminary ROI measurements and projections are created to support future SOA efforts.

The second level, *architected services*, delivers IT cost reduction and control as services are now developed and deployed in a less ad-hoc fashion. Application integration becomes more widespread. Design-time activities take center stage as architecture leadership is established. One goal at this level is to prove returns from the use of standards-based technology. A key enabler for all of these is the deployment of a comprehensive SOA education program (discussed in more detail in Chapter 10, "Acquiring the Skills for SOA").

SOA MM divides the third maturity level into two parts: *business services* and *collaborative services*. Both earmark business responsiveness as the prime business benefit. The business services side achieves this via business unit and enterprise-level business processes. The collaborative services side focuses on making services available across the enterprise and to external partners. Both depend on successful SOA life cycle governance, executive commitment, cross-organizational partnership, and event-driven design skills. Both also depend heavily on policy specification and developing an ongoing partnership between business and technology organizations. The primary difference is their scope and the technology standards that are employed.

Measured business services, the fourth level within SOA MM, is characterized by a transformation from a reactive enterprise to a more real-time strategy that is governed by well-defined business performance metrics. Critical technology success factors include business activity monitoring (BAM), complex event processing, and event-driven dashboards and alerts to empower business users with relevant and timely information. Ongoing business process evaluation and reengineering are essential from an organizational perspective.

The final phase, *optimized business services*, aims to produce an optimized business where the enterprise can react and respond automatically as circumstances change. This level employs the broadest possible scope (an entire business unit or even the whole enterprise). Event-driven automation is a critical technology success factor, enabling real-time optimizations to occur. Correspondingly, a continuous-improvement culture must emerge on the people side of things. Goals for this final phase of maturity include enterprise-wide leadership for business and SOA governance as well as proven returns for SOA-enabled continuous improvement.

Applying This Model

The SOA MM does a solid job of identifying technical and organizational business impacts of SOA adoption. It also identifies relevant standards and key goals and practices at each level. One area that is perhaps a bit shortsighted is how late governance enters the picture. Governance is a crucial risk-mitigation factor for SOA adoption and should exist, in some form, as early as possible. It can then grow over time and be adopted in an incremental fashion (much as SOA is adopted within the organization).

SELECTING A MATURITY MODEL

Although SOA has been evolving and maturing since around 2000, there are still some fairly diverse perspectives regarding the scope of SOA. Some organizations view SOA as the next evolution in distributed computing and system integration, others view SOA as the next logical step beyond component-based enterprise system design, while still others look at SOA as a paradigm shift aimed at aligning business and technology to achieve agility. Each of these viewpoints is valid. The trouble comes into play when you try to gauge the maturity of an SOA initiative. Do you gauge the maturity of the underlying technologies, the overall architecture, the business processes, or the degree to which the organization has adopted the SOA paradigm?

So, how do you select the right model for your organization? The following guidelines may help:

- Select CBDI's Web Services Maturity Model if:
  - Web Service components will comprise the bulk of your services.
  - You want a model that addresses both business and technology aspects.
  - You want a simple, phase-based maturity model.
  - Selecting a model from a company that is not selling SOA solutions is an important factor in your decision matrix.
- Select IBM's Service Oriented Integration Maturity Model if:
  - You want a model that focuses on the progression of your enterprise technology layers.
  - You want a more detailed approach to maturing your SOA.
  - Going with "Big Blue" is an important consideration for your organization.
- Select Progress-Sonic's Service Oriented Architecture Maturity Model if:
  - An explicit mapping to CMMI is important to your organization.
  - You want a model that clearly defines organizational benefits as well as success factors, goals, and practices associated with each maturity level.
  - Selecting a model developed by a consortium of vendors is an important consideration for your organization.

SUMMARY

SOA adoption is a complex process with far-reaching impacts throughout the enterprise. While there are dozens of SOA maturity models that have been defined and applied around the world, three of those models lead the pack. Each model provides a tiered, progressive approach to SOA maturity with varying degrees of emphasis on business and technology subjects. In the end, you need to select a maturity model that is right for your needs, tailor it if necessary, and then communicate and champion it throughout your organization.

NOTES

1. *Note:* There is absolutely no requirement that an organization is CMMI-compliant in order to adopt SOA, but the notion of maturity levels, tracking metrics, and process refinement is similar to CMMI. The primary difference is that there is no auditing or accreditation process associated with SOA maturity models.
2. For more information on CBDI's Web Services Maturity Model, see http://roadmap.cbdiforum.com/reports/maturity/.
3. For more information on IBM's SIMM, see www-128.ibm.com/developerworks/webservices/library/ws-soa-simm.
4. For more information on the Progress-Sonic's SOA MM, see www.sonicsoftware.com/solutions/service_oriented_architecture/soa_maturity_model.
5. The model details are available via a handy quick reference PDF from Sonic's website: www.sonicsoftware.com/solutions/docs/soamm_quick_reference.pdf.

CHAPTER 9

HOW MUCH SOA
DO I NEED?

There are some products and substances in this world for which there seem to be endless uses. Duct tape and baking soda fall into this category. What commercial, industrial, or residential malfunctions cannot be fixed with duct tape? Correspondingly, what can you not clean, disinfect, or otherwise improve with baking soda? There are, however, other products and substances that it is important that you handle more judiciously. Dynamite is very useful for mining and excavation, but no one suggests that you double the needed amount of dynamite "just to be sure." Nor would you want to use dynamite for removing every obstacle or blocked passage. Plumbing stopped up? Shove a stick of dynamite down the drain! Similarly, if you need to drive a nail into a plank of wood, then nothing works better than a hammer. If you are trying to remove the lug nuts on a car wheel, however, you will quickly get frustrated if your only tool is a hammer. In fact, when someone attempts to apply a given solution to every conceivable problem, we recite the old saying: "When all you have is a hammer, everything looks like a nail."

Service oriented architecture (SOA) is a lot more like dynamite or a hammer than it is like duct tape or baking soda. If you have a system, business process, or line of business that needs what SOA has to offer, such as interoperability, reuse, agility, and in certain cases reduced risk, then you will be *very* glad that you have the capability to employ a service oriented strategy. If, however, other drivers trump the SOA value proposition, such as performance, lower startup costs, proprietary integration, solution simplicity, rapid development with little or no oversight, or the like, then you will quickly become frustrated with an SOA approach.

This chapter explores the subject of *how much* SOA an organization really needs. Additionally, a methodology dubbed "Selective SOA™" will be presented, providing a framework for identifying and prioritizing your SOA initiatives.

SOA IS NOT A PANACEA

Contrary to the rhetoric that is floating around the Internet and various conferences, SOA is not a panacea. It is not some sort of magical tonic that is "good for what ails you." Instead, it is a powerful strategy for business and technology alignment and effective componentization of enterprise assets. In Chapter 5, "Is SOA Right for You?," we explored SOA adoption fallacies, several of which addressed this very subject. Upon examining ill-conceived service orientation initiatives across various companies and industries, some obvious patterns emerge. Exhibit 9.1 provides a list of scenarios that should send up red flags with

EXHIBIT **9.1**   *List of scenarios that identify red flags for SOA*

Service Orientation Red Flags

These aren't wrong, but proceed with caution:

- High-performance/real-time systems
- High-throughput systems
- Business-to-business interactions involving intricate transaction semantics
- Batch processes
- Data warehouses
- Any technology system or business unit where tight coupling and/or monolithic integration is desirable

respect to service orientation. It is important to realize that this list represents a huge set of generalizations. Moreover, it is merely an attempt to identify situations in which service orientation *might* be a bad fit.

The reality is that there are viable, real-world SOA implementations for each one of the items on the list (many of which the authors of this book have been involved in with various clients). However, for every success story from that list, there are 20 failures. Proceed with caution.

WHAT CHILDREN TEACH US ABOUT SOA

Children frequently teach us about the world around us without ever setting out to do so. And although I am grateful to my children for introducing me to Elmo, The Wiggles, and Dora's bottomless backpack of fortuity, I am even more grateful for what they have taught me about SOA. Specifically, they have taught me about the importance of not overapplying general rules of thumb (which children frequently do with grammar rules) and the importance of adhering to the *Goldilocks Principle* (not too hot/cold or hard/soft).

Overapplying Grammar Rules

Children's brains are like little computer programs that are constantly learning and applying rules in order to understand the world around them. As language develops, children learn and begin to apply grammar rules. In doing so, they initially apply these rules across the board. For example, a general grammatical rule in English is to add the suffix *ed* to the end of a word in order to make it a past-tense expression. This does not, however, work in every case, as the following example illustrates:

- Correct: "I *touched* the apple."
- Incorrect: "I *taked* the apple."

Over time, children learn to avoid such overapplication of grammar rules and instead apply them only where they are appropriate.

What does this have to do with the proper understanding and application of SOA? Just as children overapply grammar rules, there is a tendency for business and technology decision makers to overapply rules within the enterprise. Just because one line of business (LOB) within the enterprise has successfully deployed an SOA solution does not mean that every LOB should do so. Similarly, SOA may be better suited for certain business processes, systems and subsystems, or particular enterprise layers (i.e., infrastructure services versus domain-specific services). It is tempting to rush to apply strategies that have been successful in the past, but prudent organizations define criteria for utilizing certain strategies and continue to track the impact of decisions through verifiable metrics. These criteria and verifiable metrics should go into a decision matrix that is then managed and championed by the enterprise governance body. Choosing to utilize SOA, or any enterprise initiative for that matter, should be done on a case-by-case basis and should incorporate as much empirical information as is realistically available.

Goldilocks Principle

The second lesson that children teach us about proper service orientation comes from the popular children's story, *Goldilocks and the Three Bears*. Goldilocks was not a fan of extremes. She did not want things to be too hot/cold or hard/soft. Instead, she wanted everything to be *just right*. The same holds for SOA.

When adopting SOA, we do not want too much or too little service orientation, but we want just the right amount. At first glance, this may appear to be identical to the first lesson learned from children, but there is an important difference. If the first lesson is about recognizing that successful application of SOA in one situation does not necessarily mean that SOA is a good fit for another situation, then the second lesson is that when applying SOA to a given situation, care must be taken with respect to the extent of that service orientation. Service orient too little, and you risk not producing a solution that is sufficiently flexible or reusable. Service orient too much, and you risk overrunning your budget and adding superfluous layers of complexity. This is really a question of *right-sizing your SOA*. Identifying that a particular LOB, business process, system, or subsystem should be service oriented is the first step. The next step is to decide how much service orientation is needed to meet the requirements. You do not have to service orient all of it; you do not necessarily need everything to be a service. Additionally, you should not feel unnecessarily constrained by the reference architecture. A given solution may require more layers to increase agility or accommodate disparate data models and interfaces. Another solution may require fewer layers in order to better promote a particular reuse strategy, to keep complexity low, or to balance performance requirements. As with the first lesson, the responsibility for protecting the organization from the extremes of service orientation is placed upon the governance body. Strong business leaders and savvy enterprise architects working within the governance body should provide guidance, best practices, and a scrutinizing review of all SOA initiatives.

SELECTIVE SOA METHODOLOGY

By now, it should be abundantly clear that SOA is not the right answer for every situation. When you boil it down to the essentials, there are two reasons that SOA must be applied selectively:

1. The *expense* of service orientation cannot be recouped in every situation.
2. Service orientation can actually do more *harm* than good in certain situations.

Consequently, it is essential that the governance team put a methodology in place for determining when SOA makes sense and when it does not. The following methodology—*Selective SOA*™—has been successfully applied in a variety of SOA initiatives across different industries.

Phase 1: Bottom-Up Analysis

Selective SOA begins with a bottom-up analysis. What existing enterprise assets and resources are available for service orientation? This perspective looks at the current state of the enterprise from a people, process, and technology perspective to examine the assets and resources that are immediately available for use within an SOA. Exhibit 9.2 summarizes the key categories on which the bottom-up analysis focuses.

Typical questions that must be answered when performing a *bottom-up analysis* include:

- What current business processes could benefit from service orientation?
- What enterprise systems are available for service orientation? (e.g., customer relationship management [CRM], enterprise resource planning [ERP], custom finance package, etc.)
- What is the state of the current technology infrastructure? (e.g., hardware/software, bandwidth, networking, security, backup/restore, etc.)

EXHIBIT **9.2**   *Phase 1: Perform a bottom-up analysis*

Bottom-Up

Business Processes

Enterprise Systems

Technology Infrastructure

Organizational Assets

Available Skills

- What organizational assets are available to support this effort? (e.g., teams, staff, committees, etc.)
- What skillsets are available that could be leveraged? (e.g., object oriented [OO], XML, SOA, business process management [BPM], Information Technology and Infrastructure Library [ITIL], Six Sigma, enterprise architecture [EA], agile, etc.)

This list of questions is intended as a starting point. Ultimately, each organization must craft a list of questions that will result in a comprehensive view of the current enterprise assets and resources that are potentially available for either direct or indirect involvement in an SOA initiative.

Phase 2: Top-Down Analysis

The next phase involves a more progressive, top-down look at the enterprise. If you could start with a clean slate and reinvent your business, what would it look like? This perspective looks at the future, desired state of the enterprise from a people, process, and technology perspective. Exhibit 9.3 summarizes the key categories on which the top-down analysis focuses.

EXHIBIT **9.3** *Phase 2: Perform a top-down analysis*

Top-Down

Business Vision

New Business Processes

Next-Gen Technology

Organizational Vision

Skills Makeup

Typical questions that must be answered when performing a *top-down analysis* include:

- What business processes would enable the future state of the enterprise?
- How would the technology landscape differ if IT were given a clean slate?
- What would the organizational makeup look like in this new world?
- Describe the skills possessed by this new organization.

Once again, this list of questions is intended as a starting point. Ultimately, each organization must craft a list of questions that will result in a comprehensive view of the future enterprise that SOA should ideally help to enable.

Phase 3: Value-Based Analysis

The third phase is a value-based analysis. What elements of your business are mission critical and/or provide the most value? This perspective is a bit more subjective as each business defines value and mission-critical operations differently, but the principle remains constant. Exhibit 9.4 summarizes some of the key categories on which a value-based analysis tends to focus.

Typical questions that must be answered when performing a *value-based analysis* include:

- What transactions, products, or services produce the most revenue?
- What transactions, products, or services have the highest profit margin?
- Which systems or business processes are the most mission critical?
- What aspects of the enterprise have the most significant impact on customer service and/or customer value?
- What aspects of the enterprise do customers perceive to be most important?

EXHIBIT **9.4**   *Phase 3: Perform a value-based analysis*

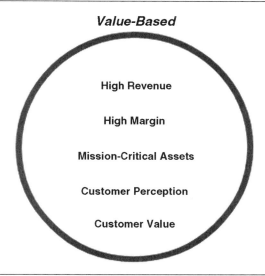

Value-Based

High Revenue

High Margin

Mission-Critical Assets

Customer Perception

Customer Value

The previous two analyses required that you tailor the list of questions to your organization, and this one is no exception. In fact, tailoring is even more important with this third analysis as it really gets at the core of what makes the business tick and what ticks customers off. Thus each organization must craft a list of questions that will correctly identify the most valuable and/or mission-critical elements of its business to ensure that SOA initiatives at least have a shot at producing a return on investment (ROI).

Phase 4: Apply the 80/20 Rule

Bottom up, top down, value based—independently, these perspectives provide only a small degree of insight regarding the proper application of SOA. It is the convergence of these three that brings to light the optimum opportunities for service orientation. Exhibit 9.5 illustrates this through a Venn diagram.

The dark-gray area in the diagram illustrates the convergence of all three forms of analysis (bottom up, top down, value based) and

EXHIBIT **9.5**   *Overlaying the bottom-up, top-down, and value-based analyses through a Venn diagram highlights candidate areas for service orientation*

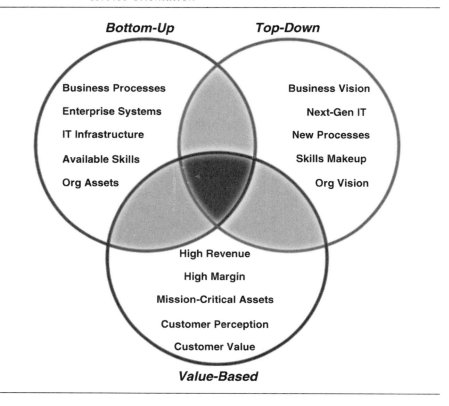

represents the best candidates for service orientation. This is the proverbial 20% of the enterprise for which service orientation will yield an 80% ROI.

> It is those high-value transactions that leverage existing skills and assets and are consistent with the long-term enterprise vision that are ideal for service orientation.

The light-gray areas in Exhibit 9.5 identify the convergence of two forms of analysis and represent the next-best candidates for service orientation:

- Those services that leverage existing skills and assets and are consistent with the long-term strategy (bottom up and top down) may not have as significant an impact on revenue and customer value, but they do represent solid opportunities for service orientation.
- Those services that leverage existing skills and assets and yield significant value for the business (bottom up and value based) represent low-hanging fruit and an opportunity for relatively quick ROI.
- Those services that are consistent with the longer-term strategy and have the potential to yield significant value (top down and value based), are important for long-term top-line growth, but tend to hold less value in the short term.

APPLYING THE SELECTIVE SOA METHODOLOGY

To see the methodology in action, we will take a look at our two case studies. Upon examination of the Return Handling and Expense Approval case studies, it is apparent that a particular element of their respective enterprises has been selected for service orientation. As such, the only real application of the methodology is a reverse-look at these cases in an attempt to validate the decision to adopt SOA. We will start with the mail-order company's Return Handling case and then proceed to explore the training company's Expense Approval case.

Applying Selective SOA to Our Mail-Order Company Case

Performing the three analyses for our mail-order company, MO1, provides some important insights:

- **Bottom-up analysis.** The affected systems and necessary technology sets already exist and are ripe for service orientation. Existing staff and skillsets can be leveraged in this initiative.
- **Top-down analysis.** The return-handling process will continue to be viable in the future state of the enterprise. The changes that

must be made to existing skills and resources in order to service orient this process are consistent with the company's long-term vision.

- **Value-based analysis.** The return-handling process does, in fact, have a material impact on company profitability as well as both real and perceived customer value.

Clearly, service orientation of MO1's return-handling process meets all three of our Selective SOA criteria:

1. Leverages existing assets and resources
2. Is consistent with long-term business vision
3. Is mission critical and/or materially impacts real or perceived business value

Applying Selective SOA to Our Training Company Case

Performing the three analyses for our training company, HighTree, provides some important insights:

1. **Bottom-up analysis.** The existing accounting system and home-grown expense management application can certainly be retrofitted to expose service interfaces (either directly or via some sort of wrapper service layer). Additionally, the expense-approval process is ripe for service orientation.
2. **Top-down analysis.** Ideally, the expense management system and manual processes would actually be replaced with a commercial product that would incur low-cost and predictable licensing fees rather than expensive in-house resources for maintenance.
3. **Value-based analysis.** While the status quo does not serve the instructors well, this business process is not mission critical and has only an indirect impact on revenue. Instructors have to become extremely frustrated with the process to refuse accepting work assignments.

Service orientation of HighTree's expense-approval process is not exactly a slam dunk. Consider how it stacks up against the three Selective SOA criteria:

1. Leverages existing assets and resources
2. Is *not* consistent with long-term business vision (preference would be to replace with a commercial product)
3. Is *not* mission critical and/or materially impacts real or perceived business value

The fact is that this particular problem can be addressed with SOA, but it is not likely to result in a positive ROI. Instead, a commercial solution along with a cursory BPM initiative should serve to address the current problems with the process. This will then free up resources to focus on other elements of HighTree's business that are better candidates for service orientation.

SUMMARY

As the old saying goes: "Less is more." With SOA, as with so many things in business and in life, it is important that it is applied judiciously. Looking to children, we learn the importance of not overapplying successful strategies and the value of getting just the right amount of something. One of the key enablers of this is an effective governance team that establishes a clear methodology and set of guidelines regarding SOA adoption. One viable approach is the Selective SOA methodology outlined in this chapter. Regardless of what methodology is utilized, the organization must strike the right balance between using SOA to try to solve everything and using it only to take advantage of low-hanging fruit. So how does an organization know what the right balance looks like? For most enterprises it takes a lot of trial and error . . . just like Goldilocks.

CHAPTER 10

ACQUIRING THE SKILLS
FOR SOA

Service oriented architecture (SOA) introduces a new mindset, new technologies, and software development tools. It is not surprising, then, that your employees will need training. What may not be so apparent is the breadth of roles that need to be trained. SOA brings the information technology (IT) and business close. Consequently, people from both sides and everyone in the middle will need some level of training in the SOA area.

A carefully developed skills-acquisition plan can train a large number of employees within a surprisingly small amount of time and budget. The key is to offer training in the right area at the right level of detail at the right time. This chapter will help you devise such a plan. First, we will identify the roles that the employees will play in business process management and SOA-based software development. Next, we will find out the kind of skills each role will need.

MULTISTAGE TRAINING PROGRAM

Instead of one huge and continuous training program, a multistage plan that educates employees in small chunks has many advantages. Some of the advantages are traditional. It is easier for people to digest small amounts of information and use them in real life before they are ready for the next level. Financially speaking, a stepped approach will help you

EXHIBIT 10.1   *As the organization becomes more mature about SOA, the general nature of the training changes*

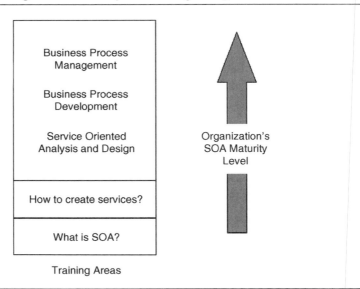

spread out the training dollars over several quarters. Some of the other advantages are purely SOA specific. An organization goes through a series of SOA maturity levels. It makes sense to have a training program that matches the current maturity level of the company while a small number of avant-garde employees get trained for the next level (Exhibit 10.1).

Personal familiarity with SOA also affects the type of training one needs. Someone who is completely new to SOA needs to understand what SOA is and learn about the benefits SOA can bring. Someone who already knows the basics needs to become an expert in the methodology and technology of SOA. In this chapter, wherever possible, we will describe a stepped training plan for each role. Each level of the step will become more vendor specific and less abstract (Exhibit 10.2). Abstract education deals with the nature of SOA and the methodology for software and business process development. Learning the key concepts of SOA without the clutter of any specific vendor's SOA tool will build the core foundation of an employee. Later, the focus should be shifted to mastering the SOA tools your organization has selected to use. Many

EXHIBIT **10.2** *Initially, SOA should be taught as a vendor-neutral abstract concept. As one gets more familiar with SOA, the focus will shift toward the vendor-specific tools*

Concrete:

• Modeling business process using vendor's tool

• Developing services and business processes using vendor's tool

• Administration and performance tuning

• Monitoring KPIs

Abstract:

• Nature of SOA

• Methodology of business process management and software development

Personal
SOA Maturity
Level

Training Areas

large organizations have more than one SOA vendor. This is where having a strong foundation in the abstract theoretical aspects of SOA really pays off. For example, a business analyst who is well familiar with the techniques of business process management (BPM) can quickly adopt any vendor's BPM tool. An analyst who knows all about a specific vendor's tool but does not know much about the methodology of BPM will be hamstrung in dealing with a complex problem.

ROLES AND RESPONSIBILITIES

Since SOA involves the business side as well as the IT, employees from many walks of the organization will play some kind of role in an SOA-based solution. In a paper titled "A Framework for Roles for

Development, Evolution and Maintenance of SOA-Based Systems,"[1] Kajko-Mattsson and colleagues have provided a detailed analysis of new roles and responsibilities that SOA will bring to an organization. The table shown here provides a simplified version of that work.

Responsibilities	Roles
Decide whether SOA is right for the organization. If so, make SOA a business principle. Drive adoption of SOA within the organization.	*SOA Leaders.* This group will be essentially made up of the executives (chief executive officer, chief technology officer, or chief information officer) and other leaders within the organization.
Perform BPM. Monitor the performance of the deployed business processes using the key performance indicators (KPIs). Drive continuous optimization of business processes.	*Business Process Managers.* This group is made up of the business managers and business analysts (BAs). BAs are trained to use BPM tools and know the methodology of BPM. Business managers know the business very well and can help the BAs define and optimize business processes.
Devise the technical infrastructure for SOA. Make sure that proper standards are being followed. Describe the technical principles (best practices). Establish the *service oriented analysis and design (SOAD)* methodology that will be used by the IT teams to design and build services.	*IT Architects*
Design and develop services and business processes. Most services will wrap existing software systems. A solid knowledge of these "legacy" systems is needed. Ideally, you want	*SOA Developers*

to have a mix of "old" and "new"
brains in this role. The new brain
will be familiar with the latest SOA
standards and development tools.

Monitor day-to-day operation of the deployed business processes. If a process instance has run into difficulty, understand the nature of the problem and devise a solution. Suggest enhancements to a business process to the business managers. Provide support to the users of a deployed business process. Accept problem reports and assist users with their work.	*SOA Support Personnel*
Test services. Test business processes.	*Software Testers*
IT governance. SOA governance.	*IT Managers*

SKILLS BY ROLE

SOA calls for new roles. That does not mean that new people have to be hired to fill these roles. Existing employees who already play a similar role will need to morph themselves into these new roles. For example, a software developer will most likely become an SOA developer and a traditional software tester will be asked to test SOA software.

Now, we will have a more detailed look at the responsibilities of each role and the skills these responsibilities demand.

SOA Leaders

Leaders need a gentle introduction to SOA and its value proposition. Usually, a one-hour session is sufficient for that. Leaders also need to learn about the potential risks of SOA and cases when SOA may not be the best choice. A degree of scepticism about SOA is a healthy attitude.

Business Process Managers

As discussed earlier, this group is made up of *business operations managers* and *business analysts*. The business managers need to learn about business process automation. They should have a clear understanding of how an automated business process functions. Next, they need to learn about how to develop a process all the way from fully manual to mostly automated. The managers will also need training on how to use the SOA vendor's tools to monitor the KPIs.

Business analysts need to know the BPM techniques in detail. They should be able to interview the business managers to learn about the current business process. They should model the business process using a software tool. Working with the business managers, they need to be able to optimize the business process. Business analysts are also responsible for defining the KPI metrics. In summary, a strong understanding of BPM and the process modeling tools are the key skills for business analysts.

The following is a suggested training plan for business analysts:

- Introduction to SOA
- Intensive training on BPM
- Business process modeling using the SOA vendor's tool

IT Architects

Architects should be able to design the technical infrastructure for SOA. This includes items like messaging, transaction management, security, reliability, and availability of the SOA software platform. For the benefit of the SOA developers, the architects should clearly answer questions like:

- How can a service consumer send a message to a service with guaranteed delivery?
- How can we encrypt communication between the service consumer and provider?

- How do we ensure that a service is up and running at all times despite potential software and hardware outage?

These issues form a foundation on top of which all SOA-based software solutions are developed. Architects must know how to build an infrastructure at an abstract and conceptual level. It is highly desirable that they also know how to actually implement the infrastructure using a specific SOA vendor's software.

Architects also keep a close eye on the rapidly evolving standards (see the Appendix, "Standards in SOA"). Some of the benefits of SOA are realized only when you follow certain standards. Architects should set clear policy for the standards that *must* be followed and the ones that *should* be followed. This policy should be revised regularly as standards mature and become more useful and as new standards become available.

Architects should also formally document how services should be identified, specified, and eventually developed. This will form the SOAD methodology for the organization. SOAD will help developers deconstruct complex problems and create a solution that is spontaneously well designed and easy to maintain.

Finally, architects should maintain a database of good and bad practices. Developers can benefit hugely from such a document.

Architects can go through a phased training program that looks like this:

- A five-day program made up of infrastructure topics (e.g., messaging, transaction, and security) at an abstract level, core SOA standards, and SOAD.
- A five-day program on how to implement the infrastructure using a specific SOA vendor's tool. A large organization may use multiple SOA platforms. In that case, an architect may decide to specialize on one platform or decide to get separate training on each platform.
- Regular self-study of the SOA standards using the published specifications of the standards.

- A short course on the administration of the SOA platform that focuses on clustering, high availability, and problem determination.

SOA Developers

Two chief responsibilities of the SOA *developer* are service development and business process implementation.

The need for a service is first identified based on the business process of a company. The specification for the services is then developed. The specification captures the nature of the tasks that the service provider is expected to perform. Next, the service is built or "coded."

A business process is modeled by the business process managers. The model is then handed over to the SOA developers, who convert the model into actual software code.

A suggested training plan for the SOA developer can look like this:

- A five-day program on the principles of service identification, specification, construction, and business process development. This class should not focus too much on any specific SOA vendor's tool. Instead, it should try to explain the nature of SOA-based software development.
- A five-day program on how to construct services and develop business processes using a specific vendor's tool. Even experienced developers will need to go through a significant learning process to pick up all the skills in this area. Specifically, development of business processes requires a new style of programming that differs from the regular procedure of object-oriented development.

SOA Support Personnel

The SOA *support team* monitors the health of the services and the business process instances. Every time a business process starts, a new instance is launched. For example, if the order fulfillment business process starts after an order is placed on the web site, every time an order is placed a new instance of the process is started. There may be hundreds or thousands of instances of a process active at any time. Most of these instances will end normally. For example, an instance of the order fulfillment process can end after the order is shipped to the customer. Many things can go wrong in the life of a process instance. Depending on the problem, the instance may terminate abruptly or may get stuck. A problematic process instance has negative impact on revenue and customer satisfaction. This is one of the drawbacks of fully automated business processes. Unless a proper plan exists for monitoring failed process instances, problems can go unnoticed for a long time, whereas for manual business processes, human employees become immediately aware of any problem.

The SOA support team is then responsible for these tasks:

- **Monitor the availability of the services.** Ideally, if a service ceases to operate, an automated monitoring system should send an alert to the support team. The team should rapidly investigate the cause of the failure and work with the system administration team to bring the service back to life.
- **Monitor the performance level of the services.** If a service starts to take longer than an expected amount of time to complete a task, an alert should be raised. The support team should investigate and resolve the problem.
- **Look for failed process instances.** Most SOA vendors provide a query tool that allows one to view instances that have failed for any number of reasons. The same tool also gives details of the failure, such as exactly what activity within the process had failed. For each failed instance, the support team should devise a strategy for resolving the situation. The solution can be as simple as resuming the instance from where it had failed. In some cases, the instance may have to be started from the beginning. In a more complex case, management will have to get involved; they will notify the affected parties and smooth out the situation.

Business process managers should be aware if any process has a tendency to fail more than the others. They can employ all kinds of countermeasures to automatically handle the failure situations. This will reduce the burden on the support staff and overall improve customer satisfaction.

- **Look for stuck process instances.** An instance can wait indefinitely for a particular task to complete. For example, in our Return Handling case study, if a staff member forgets to touch up a returned package, the associated process instance will wait forever for that task to complete. The support team should look out for such instances and devise a solution for them. It may be that the employee assigned to the task has gone on vacation. In that case, the task needs to be assigned to a different person.

Here is a suggested training plan for the SOA support team:

- A solid introduction to SOA, including the nature and purpose of services and business process.
- A five-day program on the SOA vendor's administration tool. After this program, the team should be able to perform the tasks mentioned earlier.
- A short program on the company's strategy and policy for dealing with problems with services and process instances.

Software Testers

Testing services and business processes involves unique challenges that are not present in traditional software. The *software testing team* will need new skills to understand them and create plans to deal with them.

IT Managers

IT governance in the form of ITIL (Information Technology Infrastructure Library) is not a new concept. However, it may be new within your organization. *IT managers* will need training in ITIL or similar methodologies.

The need for governance around SOA has been well established. Many believe SOA will not succeed without a well-crafted governance plan and execution of that plan. It is also believed that SOA governance needs the support of IT governance. With that in mind, we can suggest this training plan:

- Introduction to SOA
- Planning and adoption of ITIL or a similar system of IT governance
- SOA governance planning and adoption techniques

SUMMARY

SOA-based systems will need the involvement of new roles within the organization. This chapter examined these roles in details. Hopefully, this will help you plan for building a team and to make sure that they are adequately trained.

NOTE

1. Mira Kajko-Mattsson, Grace A. Lewis, and Dennis B. Smith, "A Framework for Roles for Development, Evolution and Maintenance of SOA-Based Systems," *Systems Development in SOA Environments, SDSOA '07: ICSE Workshops 2007*, 20–26 May 2007.

CHAPTER 11

RISK MITIGATION THROUGH PROPER GOVERNANCE

If you have ever been bowling, then you have likely seen children (sometimes even adults) use "bumper lanes" when bowling. That is when bars or padding are used to block bowling balls from going into the gutter. Why did they do this? The bumper lanes serve three purposes:

1. Reduce the risk of rolling into the gutters.
2. Focus on the goal (i.e., the pins at the end of the lane).
3. Increase the chance of success (i.e., hitting the pins).

Bowling provides a good analogy for risk mitigation through governance. The gutters represent areas of risk. The bumpers represent governance. Governance has three essential goals:

1. Reduce risk (i.e., project delay, cost overruns, lack of interoperability, etc.).
2. Provide focus (i.e., standards, best practices, design guidelines, etc.).
3. Increase the chance of success (i.e., on-time delivery, meet requirements, project return on investment [ROI], etc.).

Governance is not about checklists, rules, and regulations and it is not about creating a bunch of committees. Sometimes these techniques are used, but governance is more about risk mitigation by adhering to design guidelines and applying best practices. It is more of an organizational transformation and putting a framework in place to improve the probability of success. This chapter explores the subject of governance and how to effectively mitigate the risks associated with SOA adoption.

LIFE WITHOUT GOVERNANCE

Service oriented architecture (SOA) governance (or the lack thereof) is realized across three primary touch points:

1. Providing a service
2. Consuming a service
3. Supporting agreements between service provider and consumer

First we will explore the impact that a lack of governance has across these three touch points. Then we will examine how circumstances change once governance is introduced.

Touch Point 1: Providing a Service

One of the great advantages of SOA is that services are deployed into a common, standards-based environment. Client applications, other services, and even business processes can consume those services and use them as needed. This capability to reuse services in different contexts to solve business problems is a huge win in terms of information technology (IT) cost control, time to market, and overall system maintainability. The dark side of this is that in the absence of governance, any number of clients can use a service as often as they like. A service might originally have been created to support up to 150 requests per hour. Several weeks or even months after it is deployed, another business unit might decide to reuse that service in a business process that is executed up to 200 times every minute. Service performance would drop dangerously low or the service might even buckle completely and go offline.

Touch Point 2: Consuming a Service

Another tremendous advantage of SOA is that clients that consume services do not need to understand the details that exist behind the service interface. Service consumers view and treat services like *black boxes*. They are abstracted from the service implementation and unaware of the service's inner workings. While this makes it easy to consume services and insulate the consumer from changes that occur within the service implementation, it also puts the client at some risk. In the event that a service goes offline (perhaps due to lack of governance, as discussed in the first touch point), the client would then be left in a bind. The service that the client depended on is no longer working and yet the client has nothing to work with except for the service interface. There is no visibility beyond that interface and no option available for resolving or working around the failed service.

Touch Point 3: Supporting Agreements

In traditional computing, all the players and participants are very much out in the open. Components are explicitly tied together using adapters, drivers, and often specialized proprietary protocols. The very nature of the technology mandates that extensive coordination occur prior to accessing another system. All participants are able to adjust their environment accordingly to meet new demands. In a service-oriented environment, the agility and reuse can get out of hand. To guard against this, supporting agreements must be established to clearly define the responsibilities of service provider and service consumer. Furthermore, service level agreements (SLAs) are defined as well as formal communication channels in the event that a problem arises. In the absence of governance, these agreements are never formed. This leaves the utilization of SOA to be rather ad hoc and the various participants at considerable risk of service failure.

Governance Provides Order

Introducing governance across these three touch points (providing a service, consuming a service, and supporting agreements) introduces order into an otherwise chaotic environment.

Providing a Service

- Stakeholder involvement is provided throughout the service life cycle.
- Initial SLAs are established and supported with infrastructure.
- Runtime monitoring is engaged, complete with event notification.

Consuming a Service

- Service requirements, availability, and applicable policies are easily accessed via the registry.
- Formal usage requests are made, requirements are gathered, SLAs are created/updated, and the system is scaled prior to granting access.

Supporting Agreements

- End-customer needs are prioritized.
- SLAs are defined and monitored.
- Lines of communication are established to address any issues.

UNDERSTANDING SOA GOVERNANCE

SOA governance aims to provide a framework and model to manage SOA solutions in relation to managing service life cycles. It also establishes practices and lines of communication designed to facilitate collaboration and alignment with the business.

The SOA governance model should:

- Define the activities to architect, design, develop, test, and implement services.
- Define the methods employed to perform those activities, roles, responsibilities.
- Define measurement criteria to measure the success of and compliance with policies.

- Define service oriented teams, lines of communications, and best practices to facilitate alignment between business and IT.

A governance model is needed to ensure that the huge IT investments being made align with the business goals of an organization. SOA governance is primarily implemented and followed by defining procedures, policies, and metrics at various levels.

- **Procedures.** Formally identify resources and lay down processes to be followed for various activities and responsibilities assigned to various roles.
- **Policies.** These are principles that formally define the direction of a company in different areas such as security, business practices, customer support, and so forth.
- **Metrics.** These are specific indicators defined to measure the success of SOA and possibly even measure the ROI.

Beyond these three elements, guidelines and best practices are needed to promote effective service orientation. A culture of organizational transformation as well as collaborative design and development are key to successful service orientation. Once service orientation is truly adopted, it carries with it a transformational effect. It changes financial management, team staffing and organizational structure, product development life cycles, and project management.

At its core, SOA governance consists of two key best practices:

1. Documentation
   - Formally define and document roles and responsibilities.
   - Document each activity, assumption, or decision.
2. Communication
   - Communicate early and often with stakeholders at all levels.
   - Communicate across functional boundaries and include technically minded and business-minded individuals.
   - Ensure that all parties are aware of the SOA governance roles, policies, procedures, and supporting documentation.

GOVERNANCE TIPS TO SUCCESS

Risk mitigation through governance is not rocket surgery. Some try to make it terribly complex, but it is really rather simple. The following ten tips provide a recipe for successful enterprise and SOA governance.

Tip 1: Avoid extremes. As with so many things, balance and moderation are key. We want to avoid governance at the extremes:

- **Too Heavy.** Governance does not need to be a draconian enforcement of rules and regulations.
- **Too Light.** Governance does not mean adding committees.

Governance should be lean, but sufficient and provide order in a business environment.

Tip 2: Involve business stakeholders. Traditionally, IT is viewed as a dark hole into which business shovels money ("Here is some money—please keep the servers running" or "Here is some more money—I need e-mail to appear on my phone"). Effective SOA governance involves business stakeholders alongside technology subject matter experts. IT is viewed as a strategic partner to enable business, not just a cost center. Business-focused governance ensures that the SOA initiative remains grounded and focused.

Tip 3: Develop SOA champions. In order to promote a common vision for SOA and a clear understanding of the governance plan, champions must be identified and empowered to educate and motivate the organization.

How do you identify good candidates for the role of SOA champion?

- Energetic, persuasive change agents
- Visionaries that understand the current environment and how to move the organization toward a service oriented paradigm
- Facilitators that can assist the organization with understanding and utilizing the new governance framework

When selecting champions, each division or line of business should have its own champion to help its staff understand SOA's unique impact to their domain. Finally, it is important to engage the SOA champions in developing a dialogue within the organization around how to effectively govern the adoption of SOA.

Tip 4: Promote service ownership. In his seminal 1968 essay, "The Tragedy of the Commons," Garret Hardin described the dilemma associated with resources that are owned collectively.[1] If everyone owns the resource, then rational people have no incentive to expend their energy and resources to preserve and maintain the shared resource. The individual benefits immediately from the resource abuse and the consequences are distributed across the group. Hardin based his thesis on work by William Foster Lloyd, but Lloyd was not the first to make this observation. Aristotle recognized this truth centuries ago: "That which is common to the greatest number has the least care bestowed upon it."[2]

Similarly, services that do not have clearly defined ownership have a tendency to degrade over time and become less and less relevant. Services require maintenance, security updates, business rule and schema validation, and policy compliance checks. Left alone, services become less relevant, not more.

When governing SOA, service ownership is critical in order to ensure the following:

- *Accountability* to the enterprise
- *Evolution* alongside changing business needs
- *Motivation* to maintain and support
- *Quality* service and customer satisfaction

Tip 5: Govern by policy. Policies are encountered in everyday life. They represent a constraint on the use or availability of a service. Consider the following examples:

- **"No Shirt, No Shoes, No Service."** This is a common policy enforced by convenience stores and restaurants.
- **"Say please"** and **"Say thank you."** These common policies are enforced by parents on children as conditions for assistance.

Policies are used as a governance mechanism within SOA in order to constrain the use or availability of a service. If service requests comply with applicable policies, then they are permitted to transmit. Likewise, if a service is being designed or deployed into the environment, it must comply with designated policies before becoming available for use.

Examples of SOA policies include:

- Reject requests with P.O. Box addresses.
- Services will be Web Services Interoperability (WS-I) Basic Profile 1.1 compliant.
- Financial data must be encrypted.
- Text data fields must have a defined-length property.

Tip 6: Shepherd the service portfolio. Managing individual services is fine, but best-of-breed organizations look at the big picture. The entire collection of current, upcoming, and potential services must be considered, tracked, and actively governed. Shepherding an entire portfolio of services for a line of business or even the entire enterprise is key to yielding significant SOA ROI. This tends to be accomplished in two ways: service alignment with business needs, and the development and active management of a service catalog.

Business driver alignment involves taking the strategic SOA vision and aligning it with business objectives. One of the most difficult aspects of this is that business users, architects, and other SOA team members must come to a fundamental realization.

> All services are not inherently good. Services that are compliant with the organization's best practices and are consistent with the strategic direction of the enterprise are good.

This alignment is both reactive and proactive. As services are being developed or existing ones changed, they can be tweaked to be brought in line with the business. From a proactive perspective, new services can be identified and slated for development to support the enterprise's strategic SOA vision.

Service categorization is an important element of a practical portfolio of reusable services. Browsing through a handful of services is easy.

Locating the service you need out of a collection of 50, 100, or more services requires a systematic classification scheme. Taxonomies and ontologies are often used to address this need. There are various taxonomies
and ontologies from government and industry sources that can be used.
Alternatively, custom categorization methodologies can be developed (either from scratch or by extending existing methods). Regardless of what
methodology is used, define it as simply and intuitively as possible.

Tip 7: Promote a common vocabulary. "You say *potato*; I say
tomato." Service orientation means different things to different people.
As you govern the adoption of SOA, it is important that a common
understanding of service orientation, the architecture, and the enabling
infrastructure be clearly communicated. Principally, this is accomplished through the development and ongoing maturation of two documents: the SOA Reference Model and the SOA Reference Architecture.

The SOA Reference Model defines a shared vocabulary around service orientation. Common elements (i.e., Services, Policies, Data Models,
Contracts, etc.) are identified and defined, along with their dependen-
cies and interrelationships. The reference model offers a context for dis-
cussing and comparing SOA implementations. A Reference Model
provides an abstract framework and guide around best practices for architecture, governance, and business strategy alignment. A good starting point is the OASIS SOA Reference Model (SOA-RM).[3]

The SOA Reference Architecture is the embodiment of the reference
model. It takes the concepts and elements identified in the model and
gives them size, shape, and substance in the form of design patterns,
frameworks, and alignment with business requirements. It stops just
short of a concrete implementation that would include specific product/
technology stacks and specific systems and subsystems. One common
facet of a reference architecture is a clear specification regarding architectural layers (i.e., orchestration/business/application or infrastructure/
core/business unit/enterprise) complete with guidelines regarding service granularity. Two good starting points (both of which derive from
the OASIS SOA-RM) include the OASIS SOA Reference Architecture
(SOA-RA) and the Open Group SOA Reference Architecture.[4]

Tip 8: Invest in proper governance tooling. A documented governance life cycle (requirements signoff, design review, quality assurance [QA]/testing, etc.) is golden, but an automatically enforced governance life cycle is divine. Previous attempts at technology and project governance have had marginal success due to a lack of real influence over business operations. Through governance tools and supporting infrastructure such as registry/repository, policy server, service management framework, policy enforcement mechanism, and the like, governance can move from a vague concept into reality.

The governance infrastructure and tooling space has gone through some considerable evolution. Initially, service registries functioned as a glorified "yellow pages" of service information. Eventually they began to manage the service life cycle as well. Later, a whole range of governance tools emerged (service management, security enforcement, and policy management). Recently, this space has further evolved such that complete SOA governance and quality management suites have emerged. Take advantage of this in a big way. You will be glad that you did.

Tip 9: Encourage collaborative governance planning. You can force governance on teams. It will work and staff will comply with the requirements placed on them. Forcing governance on the organization has some nasty side-effects on team culture, however:

- They will do the minimum.
- They will take shortcuts.
- Some will circumvent the process and capitalize on loopholes.
- Some may even sabotage the process.

Alternatively, you can avoid the temptation to take this sort of draconian approach and instead promote a collaborative style of governance. This will tend to affect team culture in other ways:

- They will engage.
- They will innovate.
- Some may even step up to become champions of the process.

Governing collaboratively is definitely harder to do, but the results far outweigh the effort and additional time spent up front.

Tip 10: Start small and grow incrementally. If governance were a tree, you would be left with the options of either planting a seed or attempting to transplant a fully grown tree. While the latter is possible, it is fraught with difficulty. The tree is heavy; the root system must be transplanted along with the tree. A very large hole must be dug to accommodate the root system. There is a risk associated with the root system adapting to a new environment. The former option, planting a seed, certainly has its challenges (soil, water, and sunlight), but the risks are much lower and there is opportunity for it to adapt as it grows (more/less water, more/less nutrients added, etc.). Generally, organizations choose this option. They choose to start small and grow incrementally.

How governance matures will vary from enterprise to enterprise:

- It may involve a lot of infrastructure investments.
- Some governance strategies are more focused on techniques and methodologies.
- It may involve more committees and organizational changes.
- Different business units tend to be more or less bureaucratic in their governance approach.

Regardless of what form the governance takes, the key is to start small and grow incrementally. The following simple steps are recommended:

1. Define a governance roadmap with objective, measurable milestones.
2. Identify technology and organization changes required for each stage.
3. Clearly identify and document business value that is applicable at each stage.

That last recommendation is the step that is most often missed. So often organizations will put a plan of action in place without any understanding of what benefit the business will gain from each iteration or each level of maturity. This is crucial to ensuring that your SOA is relevant and that your governance is sufficient without being overkill, and ultimately is core to achieving a return on your service oriented investment.

SUMMARY

Governance is essential to successful SOA adoption and preservation of ROI. Just like the bumper lanes in bowling, governance accomplishes three things: reduce risk, provide focus, and increase the chance of success. Although standards, rules, policies, and enforcement committees are common governance elements, this is not the end of the story. Governance is as much or even more about organizational change, design patterns, guidelines, and best practices as it is about rules and regulations. To the extent that rules do enter the story, they should be clearly defined, truly objective, and automatically enforced by the infrastructure wherever possible.

SOA governance represents a crucial lynchpin in any SOA adoption strategy. Provided that it is implemented to help mitigate risk and that it is implemented incrementally according to a well-reasoned plan with milestones and clear business value at each stage, the chance of success is very high. You may not bowl a strike every time, but with proper governance, you have got a decent chance of consistently getting spares.

NOTES

1. To read the "Tragedy of the Commons" in full, consult: Garrett Hardin, *Science*, Vol. 162, No. 3859 (December 13, 1968), pp. 1243–1248.
2. For more details on Aristotle's thoughts on sharing common resources, read: *Aristotle, Politics 1261b34.*
3. To view the SOA-RM committee's efforts, check here: http://wiki.oasis-open.org/soa-rm.
4. The subcommittee documents their SOA-RA work here: http://wiki.oasis-open.org/soa-rm/ReferenceArchitecture; and http://www.opengroup.org/projects/soa-ref-arch/.

CHAPTER 12

CREATING YOUR SOA ADOPTION PLAN

By now you should have a solid understanding of service orientation as well as the advantages and disadvantages that come with it. (If you do not have a solid understanding, then you need to read the previous chapters again; but this time, try not to use the book as a replacement for your sleeping pills.) If we have successfully steered you away from service oriented architecture (SOA) adoption, then you can safely put this book down. If you are determined to move forward with adopting SOA, then this chapter is designed to assist you with crafting that plan and getting the service oriented ball rolling.

READY . . . FIRE . . . AIM?

Everyone who has been in the business world for more than six months has been involved in at least one project that was ill-conceived. Rather than taking the time-tested ready-aim-fire approach, they take a more haphazard ready-fire-aim approach.

Ready-Aim-Fire **(a solution based on defined requirements)**

- Acquiring needed resources (*ready*)
- Identifying requirements, performance metrics, and crafting a project plan (*aim*)
- Executing on the plan (*fire*)

Ready-Fire-Aim (a solution in search of a problem)

- Acquiring needed resources (*ready*)
- Rapidly moving forward to implement some new technology/methodology/technique/product (*fire*)
- Evaluating the results and then deciding what the business drivers and ultimate utilization of the project will be moving forward *(aim)*

There is a tendency for people to get overly excited about new solution sets and then look around for where they could possibly apply that solution. Many people fall into this trap with SOA. This is a recipe for disaster. The approach outlined here is intended to help business leaders to systematically guide the evaluation and pragmatic adoption of SOA. SOA is not a panacea and should not be applied haphazardly. It is a powerful enterprise architecture style that has tremendous potential to facilitate alignment between business and information technology (IT) and deliver a compelling return on your technology and organizational investments.

THE PLAN

The process of evaluating and then potentially adopting SOA involves several steps to thoroughly examine, understand, and ultimately initiate service orientation within the enterprise. These six steps are progressive, building on one another to further refine the potential for SOA and how it could benefit the enterprise in question:

Step 1: Identify the current business drivers.

Step 2: Select and initiate a pilot project to prove out SOA's potential.

Step 3: Conduct a strategic analysis regarding SOA's applicability within the business unit or the entire enterprise.

Step 4: Crystallize your SOA objectives and requirements.

Step 5: Define a detailed and incremental adoption plan.

Step 6: Communicate, educate, and collaborate across the organization.

These six steps are roughly divided into two broad categories: *SOA evaluation* and *SOA adoption*. The first three steps comprise the evaluation section. The aim is to identify SOA's applicability, if any, to the enterprise. The second set of steps focuses on the process of adopting SOA, guided by the adoption plan and roadmaps. From there, it is simply a matter of implementing the plan and fighting through the normal resistance that people put up against significant change. You know . . . the fun stuff.

EVALUATING SOA

The first three steps involve the investigation of SOA's applicability to the enterprise as depicted in Exhibit 12.1. What are the current problems and goals of the organization? How might SOA be brought

EXHIBIT **12.1** *The Six-Step SOA Evaluation and Adoption Plan guides teams through a pragmatic examination of SOA and its feasibility for a given business*

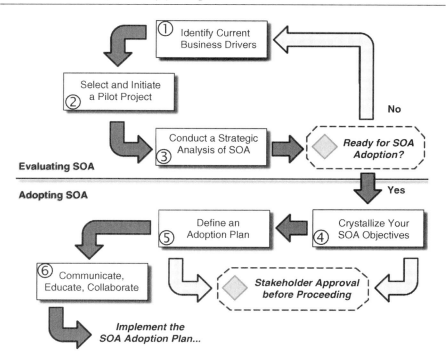

to bear to help address these issues? If the enterprise does move to become service oriented, what aspects of the business represent strong candidates?

Step 1: Identify the Current Business Drivers

Start by listing the *pain points* for the organization. The scope of the effort will dictate whether you look at a single business unit or the entire enterprise. The following questions can help to get this process started:

- Where does the group experience inefficiencies?
- Where are cost overruns occurring?
- Have there been recent project failures or significant setbacks? What were the root causes?
- Is the organization meeting all of its business benchmarks? If not, where is it coming short?
- Are the organization's information systems hitting their performance targets? If not, where is the gap?

After exploring the pain points for the group, you will flip your focus and think in terms of *growth opportunities*. Again, the scope of the effort could be a single business unit or the entire enterprise. The following questions can help to get this process started:

- What top-line and bottom-line growth targets does the group have for the year?
- What is the organization's key differentiator (i.e., speed, quality, cost, flexibility, etc.)?
- Are there any new markets, products, or services that are of strategic importance for the group?
- What is of greatest importance to the group's customers (they could be internal or external customers)?

Once you have completed the brainstorming on pain points and growth opportunities, you will look for common themes, priority objectives (i.e., which pain points or opportunities are most significant), and low-hanging fruit (i.e., which pain points or opportunities would be easiest/quickest to capitalize on). Now review Chapter 3, "SOA Value Proposition," and Chapter 6, "Applying SOA to Various Industries." Finally, ask your team one key question: "Given our current pain points and opportunities for growth, where do we see the most potential for service orientation?"

Step 2: Select and Initiate a Pilot Project

The first evaluation step walks the team through the process of identifying where the greatest potential for service orientation exists. This may be based on common themes within the pain points and growth opportunities, it may be where one or more of those are a higher priority, or it may be where the quick-wins or lowest-hanging fruits exist for SOA. The pilot project takes one of these three answers and then conducts an experimental service orientation effort as a proof of concept.

> Scoping the pilot project is critical. You need for this effort to be big enough to matter, but small enough to win.

Scope it too big, and you accept unnecessary risk; if it is too small, you risk producing a successful pilot that is inconsequential and rather trivial. The pilot project should steer clear of mission-critical processes and systems. These will be scrutinized too closely and may never see the light of day in a production environment. Trivial, peripheral processes and systems should also be avoided. Detractors will tend to discount SOA and dismiss it as expensive hype with no real business value. The sweet spot for a pilot project is to target a process or system that has a material impact on business operations and can improve the status quo in a defined and measurable way.

Step 3: Conduct a Strategic Analysis Regarding SOA's Applicability

With the pilot project complete, the team should have clearer idea regarding SOA's potential within the organization. Now it is time to conduct a formal, strategic analysis regarding where and to what extent service orientation makes sense for the organization. While there are several approaches that might be taken, the Selective SOA™ methodology introduced in Chapter 9, "How Much SOA Do I Need?," is the recommended approach.

As a quick refresher, the *Selective SOA* methodology involves three forms of analysis, followed by a synthesis of the results:

- **Bottom-up analysis.** What existing enterprise assets and resources are available for service orientation? This perspective looks at the current state of the enterprise from a people, process, and technology perspective to examine the assets and resources that are immediately available for use within an SOA.
- **Top-down analysis.** If you could start with a clean slate and re-invent your business, what would it look like? This perspective looks at the future, desired state of the enterprise from a people, process, and technology perspective.
- **Value-based analysis.** What elements of your business are mission critical and/or provide the most value? This perspective is a bit more subjective as each business defines *value* and *mission critical operations* differently, but the principle remains constant.
- **Synthesize the results.** Bottom up, top down, value based—independently, these perspectives provide only a small degree of insight regarding the proper application of SOA. It is the convergence of these three that brings to light the optimum opportunities for service orientation.

Selective SOA sheds light on the proverbial 20% of the enterprise for which service orientation will yield an 80% ROI. It is those high-value transactions that leverage existing skills and assets and are consistent with the long-term enterprise vision that are ideal for service orientation.

At the conclusion of this third step, the project stakeholders have an important decision to make. Should the team be given a green-light to move into the SOA adoption phase? By looking at the results of the first three steps, a realistic picture of service orientation and its applicability to the organization can be clearly understood. The stakeholders must decide in which direction to go next.

This decision point for the stakeholders is depicted in Exhibit 12.1. If the current perspective and approach to service orientation is not favorable, then the stakeholders can either approve a reiteration of the first three steps, or cancel the effort altogether. If the current perspective and approach are favorable, then they can approve the progression from SOA evaluation to SOA adoption.

ADOPTING SOA

Provided that the first three steps result in a green light for SOA, then the final three steps define and ultimately implement an SOA adoption plan. What metrics will be used for gauging SOA success? How will ROI be calculated? What incremental steps and corresponding milestones will be used? How will the initiative be communicated and other stakeholders brought in to support the plan?

Step 4: Crystallize Your SOA Objectives and Requirements

At this point in the process, it is time to collect, refine, and document your requirements regarding SOA adoption. There must be agreement within the team and the project stakeholders regarding what adopting SOA will accomplish, what metrics will be used to measure success or failure, and what figures and formulas will be employed for gauging the ROI for SOA initiatives. Chapter 7, "Calculating SOA ROI," will provide assistance with that last item, but the first two must be accomplished using standard discovery techniques (use cases, agile stories, process modeling, stakeholder interviews, collaborative brainstorming, etc.).

It is critical that the results of this step be physically documented, approved by the stakeholders, and configuration controlled. When moving out of SOA evaluation and into SOA adoption, organizations tend to find considerable value in taking a more disciplined and in some cases formal approach to the whole process. Evaluating SOA as a possibility still includes multiple opportunities to jettison the project with minimal impact on the business. Once the adoption process has begun, however, considerable resources are brought into play and other projects and initiatives are potentially impacted. For this reason, it is important that requirements are clearly spelled out, along with the criteria for success and the mechanisms in place for calculating the relative value or benefit provided by SOA.

Step 5: Define a Detailed and Incremental Adoption Plan

The fifth step consists of two fundamental activities: selecting a maturity model and then crafting one or more roadmaps for SOA adoption. The maturity model provides a way to identify and track the state of service orientation from both a technology and business perspective. Roadmaps are used to define incremental steps and objective milestones for maturing SOA within the organization over time.

To begin with, a maturity model should be selected. Chapter 8, "Selecting an SOA Maturity Model" goes into great detail on this topic. Once you have selected a maturity model (or defined your own), the next step is to produce a roadmap based on that model. That roadmap should accomplish three things:

1. Identify where you are today.
2. Recognize what phases or levels of maturity you may have already completed.
3. Plan milestones and deliverables for progressing to higher levels of maturity.

In developing a model and corresponding roadmap for your organization, multiple elements come into play. Several facets of the enterprise are examined in order to capture the current and future states and ultimately to facilitate the creation of roadmaps to enable change:

- **Business maturity.** Business responsiveness, strategic alignment, performance management, and so on

- **Architecture maturity.** Network and application topology, design patterns, technical infrastructure, and so on
- **Technology maturity.** Protocol and messaging standards, design and development techniques, application platforms, operating systems, databases, and so on
- **Organization maturity.** Organizational structure, knowledge and skills, training programs, project planning, staffing plans, and so on
- **Governance maturity.** Funding models, roles and responsibilities, policy definition and enforcement, life-cycle management, governance model, and so forth

Each of these facets of enterprise maturity can be tracked independently and roadmaps with objective milestones established to guide the evolution of the enterprise from the current state to the future state. Tracking the maturity of these various facets independently is important because they will not all progress at the same rate. In planning and strategizing around these elements, you can either create one comprehensive model and roadmap (matrix style) or create five separate ones (linear style).

As with the previous step, the results of this planning (maturity model selected, roadmap(s) defined, milestones and metrics, etc.) should be documented, configuration-controlled, and approved by the stakeholders before proceeding.

Step 6: Communicate, Educate, and Collaborate across the Organization

The evaluation of SOA is complete and SOA adoption has been approved. Requirements have been gathered, expectations clearly defined, and a detailed adoption plan has been defined and approved. This leads to the final step—communicate, educate, and collaborate.

It is time to engage the rest of the business unit or even the entire enterprise in embracing SOA and the adoption plan that will be put in motion. This involves communicating the vision or mission for service orientation and describing the pilot projects and lessons learned. Additionally, an SOA education program must be in place covering a broad spectrum of roles (executive, senior management, line management, architect, designer, tester, developer, administrator, and governor). Finally, a dialogue around service orientation (complete with collaboration/community software like a wiki) should be developed in order to foster discussion and critical thinking around service orientation and how it applies to the organization, business partners, and ultimately customers.

SUMMARY

Service orientation can be pragmatically evaluated and then adopted. Evaluating SOA begins by identifying the current drivers and goals that are motivating the business. Next, a pilot project is launched to explore SOA's potential to support these drivers. The evaluation process concludes with a high-level, strategic analysis regarding SOA's viability to address the business objectives. At this point, the organization can either accept SOA and move toward adoption, or revisit the evaluation phase, or shelve SOA adoption plans entirely. Assuming that the evaluation phase resulted in a positive view of SOA's viability, then the organization can proceed to crystallizing the objectives and requirements, defining a detailed adoption plan, and finally communicating and collaborating with all levels of the organization regarding the plan. Once this is complete, then it is simply a matter of enacting the plan and tracking the results.

NEXT STEPS

That is it; you are well on your way. Once you enact that sixth step, you are ready to actually execute the plan and make it happen. As you work through those six steps and even beyond, there are a number of resources that we recommend for additional education, mentoring, support, and guidance:

- **SOAmatters.com.** Kyle Gabhart's blog and SOA resource site (blog, links to articles and tutorials, links to case studies, links to SOA standards, etc.)
- **WebAgeSolutions.com.** Education and Mentoring portal (knowledge base, customized instructor-led training, project-based mentoring, etc.)

We wish you all the best on your SOA journey. Service orientation is a bold move that holds the potential to dynamically transform your organization, product/service line, information systems, and more. Whether you are changing your business to become more efficient, more responsive, or more innovative, service orientation is a powerful tool that can be brought to bear. It is not an easy journey. After all, people resist and fear change (information systems are not exactly eager to change, either). But with a solid plan and a committed team, you can do anything!

STANDARDS IN SOA

The attempt to standardize nearly all aspects of communication between two software applications is a major contribution of service oriented architecture (SOA). Such attempts are not new. In computer science, the discipline that deals with *intersoftware communication* is known as *distributed computing*. The history of distributed computing dates back to the 1970s. Notably, two standardization efforts—DCE/RPC and CORBA—stand out from the crowd. They provided a reliable way to send data from one application to another. The applications did not have to be developed using the same programming language or have to be running on the same operating system. This principle, that any software should be able to exchange data with any other software, irrespective of their architecture, programming language, or operating system, is known as *interoperability* (Exhibit A.1). Interoperability is a key goal of distributed computing.

DCE/RPC and CORBA were comprehensive, and allowed one to develop enterprise-scale solutions. They were also supremely complex. Their complexity prevented vendors from properly following them in their products. These standards were created and maintained by a consortium of vendors. Differences in view and a general lack of cooperation among the vendors slowed down any intelligent growth and adaptation of these standards (a condition that is disparagingly known as "design by committee"). In the end, despite all the sophistication, the market failed to adopt these standards.

Later, Microsoft came up with a distributed computing technology, known as DCOM. This was completely Microsoft and Windows proprietary. A technology that is controlled by a single vendor has the advantage of being agile on its feet. But, that is no compensation for the fact that a software running in mainframe could not easily use DCOM to communicate with a programming running in Windows.

EXHIBIT **A.1**   *Distributed computing makes it possible for any software to interact with any other software over the network*

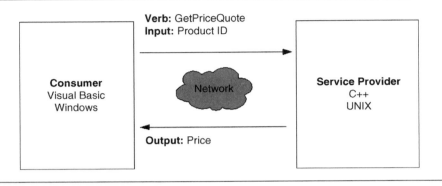

In the mid-1990s, Sun proposed a new standard known as Enterprise Java-Bean (EJB). EJB was built on top of CORBA but hid many of the complexities from the developers. EJB had two deep flaws. It was still unnecessarily complex. More important, the EJB standard was restricted to the Java programming language. A program written in COBOL, for example, could not communicate with a program written using C++. To make things even worse, people soon found out that the interoperability between different vendors' EJB platforms was fragile and fraught with many roadblocks.

At this bleakest moment for distributed computing, Microsoft introduced SOAP (Simple Object Access Protocol). SOAP, in its basic form, is utterly simple and positively lowbrow compared to CORBA or DCE/RPC. This simplicity drove widespread adoption of the standard. To this day, no other distributed computing standard has enjoyed the same level of interoperability as SOAP.

SOAP is simple, and a great starting point for communication between software applications. But, a robust distributed computing model demands more features. For example, we need to be able to encrypt the messages between the applications. The beauty of SOAP is that you can keep adding extra features in layers. Each additional feature is covered by a standard that builds on top of SOAP. This helps one to start small and add more robustness as needed. Exhibit A.2 will give some idea of how this works.

ADOPTING STANDARDS IN YOUR ORGANIZATION

Not all standards are useful for everyone or applicable to all scenarios. You should at least know what a standard can do for you. You can then decide if it is important for the services in your organization to follow that standard.

EXHIBIT **A.2** *In SOA, standards are layered. You use only what you need*

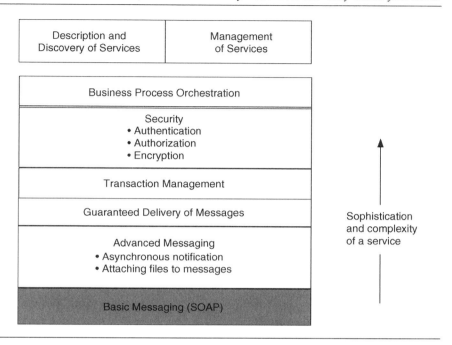

A newborn standard is often immature. By that I mean that it may not address all scenarios. Also, it takes a while for the vendors to support a standard in their SOA platform. In its more mature state, a standard is supported by most vendors and is interoperable among the vendors.

In summary, before adopting a standard, make sure that:

- It solves your problems.
- It is supported by your SOA vendor.
- It is sufficiently interoperable among the vendors.

MAINTAINER OF STANDARDS

We can see a pattern in the way SOA standards are formed and then maintained. In the beginning, a group of vendors get together and formulate a standard. For example, the Web Services Addressing standard was formed by IBM, BEA Systems, Microsoft, SAP AG, and Sun Microsystems.

Later, the standard can be passed on to a formal council. For example, OASIS (Organization for the Advancement of Structured Information Standards) maintains a large number of Web Services standards. Some of the standards are also being maintained by W3C (World Wide Web Consortium).

MESSAGING STANDARDS

SOAP 1.2

SOAP is one of the foundational standards of SOA. Many other standards build on it. It stipulates the format of the messages exchanged between the applications.

SOAP requires that all messages be formatted according to XML. For example, an application requesting a price quote can formulate a request message as follows:

```
<Envelope>
<Body>
  <GetPriceQuote>
    <ProductId>41</ProductId>
  </GetPriceQuote>
</Body>
</Envelope></codeDisplayEnhanced>
```

The service provider application, upon receiving this request message can send a reply back as follows:

```
<Envelope>
<Body>
  <GetPriceQuoteResponse>
    <Price>32.95</Price>
  </GetPriceQuoteResponse>
</Body>
</Envelope>
```

Web Services use SOAP as the message format. In SOA, not all services are Web Services and consequently you do not have to use SOAP. However, to make your services interoperable, Web Services are an excellent choice. At minimum, services that you intend to expose to your customers, suppliers, and partners should be highly interoperable.

SOAP concerns itself only with the format of the messages. It does not stipulate exactly how the messages will be delivered. Today, most SOAP messages are exchanged using the HTTP protocol, the same protocol used by the Web browsers and Web servers. There is nothing stopping you from sending a SOAP message via e-mail, or simply by saving the message in a file.

Web Services Addressing

Exhibit A.3 shows an example of how two software applications can engage in a conversation. It is possible that it may take a few days for the seller to prepare a price quote. In that case, the buyer-side application should not wait after sending the request. Once the price quote is ready, the seller should contact the buyer and send the quote. This type of interactive communication is called *conversation*. In this example, there are two separate interactions taking place. Each interaction has a request and acknowledgment message.

Conversation is an important pattern and highly recommended in situations where the service provider cannot immediately service a request. However, conversation brings in a few extra problems that plain SOAP messaging cannot cope with:

- The service provider must know the address of the consumer. This helps the service provider contact the consumer when the reply message is ready for sending. In our example, the seller may be getting price quote

EXHIBIT **A.3** *Conversation between two applications*

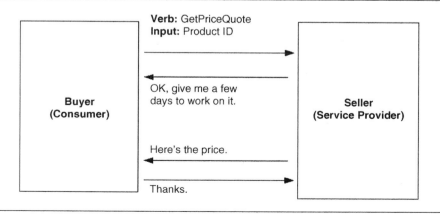

requests from many different organizations. It is important that the price quote reply goes back to the right buyer.

- The reply message must be correlated with the request. The consumer organization may have sent many price quote requests. Once it gets a reply, it must be able to tell which request it corresponds to.

The **Web Services Addressing** standard extends basic SOAP to solve these problems. Essentially, the initial request message contains an address where the reply can be sent. The message also contains a unique message ID. The reply message includes this message ID. This way, the consumer can get the reply and correlate that with the original request.

ADVANCED STANDARDS

Web Services Notification

Both plain SOAP messaging and Web Services Addressing suffer from a few limitations. The consumer must be aware of the address of the service provider. Also, the request message is sent to only one service provider. This type of one-to-one messaging cannot easily solve certain problems where there are potentially several service providers (Exhibit A.4).

EXHIBIT **A.4**   *In some cases, the same message needs to be sent to a number of service providers*

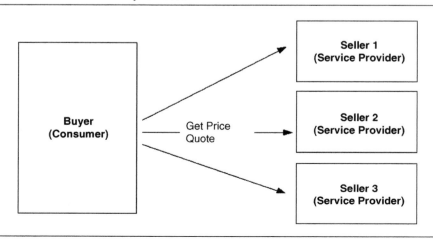

Any savvy buyer organization will send the price quote request to multiple sellers. Competition for price is the main reason for it. Also, not all buyers will have the product in stock. It is only prudent to contact several buyers. In a situation like this, it would be ideal where the buyer-side application did not have an intimate knowledge of the number and location of the seller service providers. These things should be configured outside of the consumer application.

Web Services Notification extends SOAP to make that possible. It allows the service providers to subscribe to certain events. When these events take place, the consumer publishes a message. All service providers that are interested in that message are then notified.

Web Services Reliable Messaging

When an application sends a SOAP message using the HTTP protocol, there is no guarantee that the receiver will get the message. At minimum, two things can go wrong. The network may be down, or the receiver application may not be running to accept the message. IT has used the ensured delivery pattern to solve this problem. **Web Services Reliable Messaging** extends SOAP to achieve the same.

For critical business applications, it is highly recommended that you consider reliable messaging. It is interesting to note that Web Services Reliable Messaging does not restrict itself to any specific protocol. That means that if your SOA vendor supports it, you may be able to guarantee message delivery over simple protocols like HTTP, even though it was not originally designed for that.

Transaction Management

Exhibit A.5 presents a scenario where a business process asks the accounting system to send an invoice to a customer and then asks the warehouse to ship the order. It is possible that the warehouse will fail to complete the task (perhaps the items are out of stock). In that situation, we have an inconsistent state of affairs. The buyer will not be very happy to receive an invoice for an order that will never ship.

Traditionally, this problem has been solved using a concept called *transaction*. All tasks done within the scope of a transaction either complete successfully or are completely undone if at least one task fails. When all the work is undone, the state of affairs goes back to the original state before the transaction started. In SOA, we continue to use transaction, but with a new catch. A business process

EXHIBIT **A.5**   *Transaction helps undo all the work done in a business process*
when any task fails

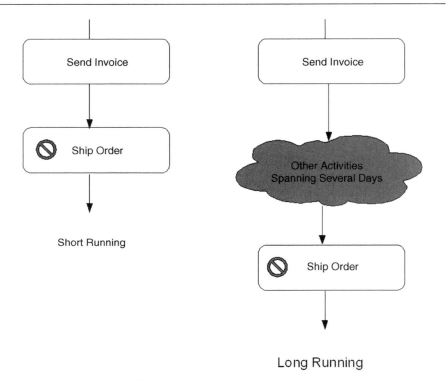

can run for many days or weeks. Transaction technology assumes that all tasks will be done in a very short period of time. Traditional transaction technology will run into problems when the collection of tasks runs for a long time. (The details of why that is the case are beyond the scope of this book.)

SOA proposes three separate standards to provide a comprehensive solution to all of these problems. The **Web Services Coordination** standard is the main one and covers the core problems that apply in all scenarios. The **Web Services Atomic Transaction** standard covers the scenario where tasks are short-lived. In this case, the standard uses traditional transaction management.

Undoing a long-running transaction is a complex matter. Traditionally, a concept called *compensation* has been used. According to that, every task has one or more compensatory tasks. If the transaction needs to be undone, these compensatory tasks are executed for each task that had successfully completed within the long-running transaction. In SOA, the **Web Services Business**

Activity attempts to standardize this behavior. A service built according to this standard will know how to undo its work. If a transaction needs to be compensated, a transaction coordinator asks the service to compensate for its work.

Web Services Security

At a minimum, you need to address three aspects of security:

1. **Authentication and authorization.** This restricts access to certain services to authorized users or business organizations.
2. **Confidentiality.** This encrypts messages so that only the intended target of a message can read it.
3. **Nonrepudiation.** This proves with a high degree of mathematical certainty that a message was sent by a specific party (organization or user) and that the message was not altered by anyone. For example, if a company sends a message to place an order, they cannot claim that they never sent that message or that someone had changed the message.

The **Web Services Security** (WS-Security) standard attempts to cover these topics. This standard is currently being managed by OASIS.

Authentication is a complex problem in a distributed environment. A message may need to be routed by a liaison application or a message may need to be sent on behalf of another organization. In all cases, the identity of the sender needs to be sent along with the message. For example, when a company places an order, the seller needs to send a message to the buyer's accounting system. If the accounting system restricts access to the buyer organization only, the seller must send the message as the buyer. A whole slew of standards are being proposed to solve this problem of identity propagation. **Web Services Federation Language, WS-Security Kerberos Binding,** and **Security Assertion Markup Language** (SAML) are some of them.

BUSINESS PROCESS ORCHESTRATION STANDARDS

Having a standard way to define a business process has several advantages:

- You can use best-of-breed tooling to model your business process. Later, you can execute that process in your SOA vendor's platform.
- You can easily hire resources. If a resource knows the standard, it will be relatively easy for her to get up to speed with your SOA vendor's implementation of the standard.

Web Services Business Process Execution Language (WSBPEL, or simply BPEL) is the primary standard for defining a business process. The latest version is 2.0. It is currently being maintained by OASIS.

WSBPEL was primarily designed for fully automated interaction between services. It did not directly address situations where services are rendered by human beings. Several SOA vendors came up with their own approach for allowing a WSBPEL process to interact with human services. As of 2007, two standards have emerged in this area. **Web Services Human Task** (WS-HumanTask) provides a way to define a human task. **WS-BPEL Extension** extends WSBPEL and provides a way to execute the human tasks from a business process.

SERVICE MANAGEMENT STANDARDS

We have a few standards that are trying to provide a uniform way to manage a service after it has been put into production. Management tasks include:

- Check to make sure that a service is up and running.
- View the performance statistics of a service.
- View the usage statistics of a service.
- Let a service notify an agent when it is experiencing problems.

In SOA, where you have services running in several different vendors' platforms, it may be hard to track down the source of a problem. A standardized interface for management will foster development of management tools that can work with many different SOA platforms.

The **Web Services Distributed Management** (WSDM) is attempting to standardize management. It has two parts. First, **Management Using Web Services** (MUWS) provides a way to manage any generic resource. A resource can be a television set or a remote weather station. Second, **Management of Web Services** (MOWS) extends MUWS when a Web Service is a resource that needs to be managed.

CONCLUSIONS

Earlier attempts at standardizing distributed computing met with limited success. Web Services changed all that. The level of cooperation among vendors and the practical interoperability that we are seeing today are unprecedented.

The industry is taking advantage of this momentum by extending the scope of standardization. From simple SOAP-based messaging, we now have gone to standard vendor-neutral ways of providing security, transaction, and guaranteed delivery. In the end, these additional standards are not a luxury but a necessity for a robust IT environment. The success of SOA will depend on them.

INDEX

Adoption:
  best practices, 70–71,
  case studies (*See* Case Studies)
  evaluating, 102–105, 200–205,
    208
  governance of, 197–198. *See
    also* Governance
  maturity (*See* Maturity Models)
  of service standards, 212–213
  pilot project (*See* Pilot Project)
  planning, 196, 199–201,
    205–208
  risks, 162–165. *See also* Risks
  roadmap, 197, 201,
    206–207
  selective (*See* Selective SOA)
Agility. *See* Value Proposition
Automation. *See* Value
    Proposition

Business Case, 101–106. *See also*
    Case Studies
Business Process, 17–21, 29–30,
    33–36, 48–57, 74–75,
    79–80, 217–220

Business Process Execution
    Language (BPEL). *See*
    Standards
Business Process Management
    (BPM), 17, 29, 33, 68, 78,
    88, 111, 178, 180
  definition, 33
  KPIs (*see* Key Performance
    Indicators)
  modeling (*see* Process
    Modeling)
  monitoring, 51–54, 183–184
  simulation, 46–48
Business Value. *See* Value
    Proposition

Calculated Reuse Model, 130,
    132–133
Case Studies, 13–27, 42, 51, 53,
    71–72, 80–81, 136–137,
    171–173, 184
  customization of, 119–121
  defense sector, 107–110
    intelligence community,
    108–109

Case Studies (*Continued*)
  simulation industry,
    109–110
  financial sector, 110–113
    banking and investment
      industries, 110–112
    insurance industry, 112–113
  media sector, 113–115
    broadcasting and publishing
      industries, 114
    digital and new media
      industries, 114–115
  technology sector, 115–117
    e-commerce industry,
      115–116
    telecommunications industry,
      116–117
  travel sector, 117–119
    airline industry, 118
    railroad industry, 118
    automobile industry, 119

Education. *See* Training
Enterprise Application Integration
  (EAI), 34–35, 78, 91, 97,
  149, 152–153. *See also*
  Integration
Enterprise Architecture (EA),
  143–144

Governance:
  adoption, 197–198
  best practices, 191–197
  by policy, 193–194

champions, 192–193
  extremes, 192
  maturity models (*See* Maturity
    Models)
  model, 190–191
  service ownership, 193
  service portfolio, 194–195
  stakeholder involvement, 192
  tooling, 196
  touch points, 188–190

Integration, 59–60, 71–72, 75, 85,
  97, 113, 120, 144–147,
  149–153, 157–158
Iterative Reuse Model,
  130–132

Key Performance Indicators
  (KPIs), 21, 32–33, 41,
  53–54, 78, 178, 180

Legacy Systems, 8, 85–86, 93,
  112–113, 129, 150, 156,
  178. *See also* Monolithic
  Systems
Loose Coupling, 50, 60, 111, 115,
  129, 150

Maturity:
  architectural, 207
  business, 147, 206
  governance, 197, 207
  models (*see* Maturity Models)
  organization, 175–177, 207

service, 24–26
standards, 212–214
technology, 207
training levels, 175–176
Maturity Models:
Capability Maturity Model
Integrated (CMMI),
143–144
gauging, 144, 206–207
selecting, 158–159
Service Integration Maturity
Model (SIMM), 148–153,
159
Service Oriented Architecture
Maturity Model
(SOAMM), 154–159
Web Services Maturity Model,
145–148, 159
Monolithic Systems, 5–7, 64–65,
68, 151, 162

Orchestration. *See* Business
Process

Policy, 149, 155–156
compliance, 190–192
governance (*see* Governance)
infrastructure, 10–11
management, 89–90
Pilot Project, 128, 155–156, 200,
203, 208
Process Modeling, 39–48

Quality Assurance. *See* Testing

Return On Investment (ROI), 101,
125, 198, 205
calculation, 128, 130–138
operational, 129–133
quantification of, 126–127
strategic, 134–135
tactical, 127–129
Reuse:
governance, 188–189
maturity of, 24–26
models (*see* Calculated Reuse
Model, Iterative Reuse
Model)
ROI, 129–133, 136–138
risks, 80–82, 188–189
value, 55, 59, 62–64, 112,
127
Risk(s):
agility, 87–88
industry immaturity, 89–91
integration, 85–87
process automation, 79–80
quality, 76, 92
reduction of, 66–68, 187–188
tolerance, 135–136
service composition, 82–85
service reuse, 80–82
Roadmap. *See* Adoption

Selective SOA™, 162, 165–173,
204
Service: *See also* Web services
abstraction, 56–57
composition, 82–85

Service (*Continued*)
  contract, 6
  definition of, 9
  endpoint, 50
  interface, 49, 71, 100–101, 172,
    189
  layer, 8–9
  lifecycle, 6, 11, 155–157,
    190–191, 196
  orchestration (*see* Business
    Process)
  ownership (*see* Governance)
  performance, 99–100, 188
  portfolio, 69, 194–195
  reuse (*see* Value Proposition)
Service Level Agreement (SLA), 4,
    6, 9, 11, 117, 189–190
Service Orientation, 7, 11–13,
    37–39, 208–209
Service Oriented Architecture
    (SOA):
  architecture, 7–9
  champions for, 192
  concept, 3–6
  definition, 7
  evolution, 11–12
  infrastructure, 10–11
  layers, 8–9
  maturity (*see* Maturity)
  governance of (*see* Governance)
  planning for (*see* Adoption)
  Reference Model, 195
  Reference Architecture,
    195

Stakeholders, 39–41, 190–192,
    204–205, 207
Standards, 211–221
  adoption of, 212–213
  BPEL, 41, 49, 220
  SOAP, 82, 85–86, 89, 98,
    115, 156, 214–217,
    221
  WSDL, 156 (*see also* Service
    Interface)
  XML, 12, 70, 82, 85–86, 89, 98,
    100, 109, 111, 115, 145,
    156, 167, 214

Testing, 66, 76, 92–93, 103, 184,
    196
Training, 31–33, 99, 156–157,
    200, 207–208
  multistage, 175–177
  reskilling, 54, 99
  responsibilities, 177–179
  by role, 179–185

Value Proposition:
  agility, 59, 64–65, 67–68,
    71, 126–127, 134–135,
    165
  alignment, 68, 78, 127, 146,
    194–195, 206
  automation, 18, 21, 23, 38, 80,
    98, 100–101, 157–158,
    180
  cost reduction, 47, 59–62, 88,
    112, 129

modernization, 69–70
reuse (*See* Reuse)
risk reduction, 66–68
time-to-market, 69,
    113
visibility, 69

Web Service(s), 11–12, 60, 82,
    85–87, 90, 98–99, 102,
    105, 145, 148, 159,
    215–220

XML. *See* Standards